Our Little Secret

Our Little Secret

Duncan Fairhurst

HODDER &
STOUGHTON

Copyright © 2007 by Duncan Fairhurst

First published in Great Britain in 2007 by Hodder & Stoughton
A division of Hodder Headline

The right of Duncan Fairhurst to be identified as the Author
of the Work has been asserted by him in accordance
with the Copyright, Designs and Patents Act 1988.

A Hodder & Stoughton Book

1

A CIP catalogue record for this title is available from the British Library

Hardback ISBN 978 0 340 93268 1
Trade paperback ISBN 978 0340 93522 4

Typeset in Sabon by Hewer Text UK Ltd, Edinburgh
Printed and bound by Clays Ltd, St Ives plc

Hodder Headline's policy is to use papers that are natural, renewable
and recyclable products and made from wood grown in sustainable forests.
The logging and manufacturing processes are expected to conform
to the environmental regulations of the country of origin.

Hodder & Stoughton Ltd
A division of Hodder Headline
338 Euston Road
London NW1 3BH

Acknowledgements

My thanks first of all to David Riding, Jeff Hudson, Rowena Webb and Helen Coyle, who all helped make this book possible.

A very big 'thank-you' to Shy Keenan, Chief Advocate of Phoenix Survivors. She listened when others didn't and stopped me from going mad. Shy, you are an inspiration to me.

There are too many significant people to thank all of them here. However the most important are: Ashley '50p Man', Shelly Palmer, John Owens, Wrecks, Rosalie Clothier, Nicola Jones, Roger Jones, Jo & Graham, Mark Nixon and James Green, Tim Gross, Liverpool Ste, Bushy, Biker Daz, Etienne Verstraelen, Steve Pugsley, Mark Gould, Ken'ichi Tomono and, finally, my therapist Derrick Williamson.

Without you all I wouldn't be alive today. That is a fact, not an exaggeration.

Finally, thank you to those invisible people, who without reservation fight the scourge of paedophilia that is rampant in our society.

To those who have suffered as I have, I say this: find a way to tell, speak out, keep fighting and shout as loud as you can until somebody listens.

It's our duty to protect others and to stop the guilty from going free.

Some of the names in this book have been changed to protect the individuals concerned. The facts, I'm afraid, are painfully true.

Dedication

To my wife Chie, whose love keeps me strong.
Also to my adopted brother Big Dave, whose loyalty
and friendship during my father's trial helped me
through the toughest period of my life.

Foreword

Duncan Fairhurst paid dearly for doing the right thing. His journey was made so much harder than it ever needed to be – by the powers that be. I am extremely proud of Duncan, who is not so much a victim or survivor, more a survival in progress – what we like to call a true Phoenix.

It has always been so difficult to explain to those who have never walked in our shoes exactly what it is like to be forced to live through such an abnormal, vile, corrupting and abusive childhood, within what looks to everyone else to be a very normal and ordinary life.

Equally difficult is trying to explain to non-victims how you can experience such horrifying abuse and just not know it for what it is. The only way I have ever found to help others even approach understanding this, was to ask them to imagine being told, that without any doubts whatsoever, simply watching TV means that you are the victim of child sexual abuse. In order for this to work, you really have to pretend that doing something as innocent, ordinary and mundane (and often with or in front of friends and family) as watching TV, actually makes you a victim. Then, just try to imagine exactly how that realisation would impact on everything you had so far known, understood, accepted or believed in.

With breathtaking, heart-stopping honesty, Duncan lets you into our most private, emotional inner sanctum and gives you the best insight I have ever come across into how that terrible reality can indeed come to be.

Duncan's brave and courageous journey back to his past was made to keep other children safe from the same fate and to rescue his own future from the abnormal, selfish and perverted adult who stole his childhood from him. Along the way he has helped many a Phoenix rise from very similar ashes. Duncan came to us for help and ended up inspiring us all.

Shy Keenan
Chief Advocate, Phoenix Survivors

Contents

INTRODUCTION

I Am a Survivor

I think if he had been alone that day, I would have murdered him there and then.

He was an old man. I was bigger than him. I could have punched him once from where I stood and he would have fallen into the moving traffic. My mind raced with the possibilities and I felt the adrenalin surge through my body as I stood, rooted to the spot, watching him. For ten years I had been dreaming about what I would do if I ever saw him again. Now, out of the blue, here was my chance. But I did nothing.

Because I had seen the boy.

The old man, dressed in a pale blue shirt and black Adidas tracksuit bottoms, was holding hands with a dark-haired young lad, no more than five years old. To the world at large they must have looked like any other happy family members walking through Grantham that day, but my sto-mach turned. The old man looked like the cat that got the cream. He was too engrossed in his young companion to notice anything else, not even when he walked within three feet of his own son.

Me.

But I only needed a second to recognise him.

I had no idea who the boy was – I still don't know – but I knew I couldn't do anything while he was there. I didn't need a name to know the kid had already suffered enough. When you've been abused you can spot it in others.

So I let the old man – my old man – pass. I let him brush almost against me, and even though my skin prickled with cold hatred I didn't yell in his face all those speeches I had been reciting in my head for so long. About how close to death I have come on so many occasions because of what he did to me. About the thousands of pounds – probably hundreds of thousands, and mostly of other people's money – I have spent on drugs to block out the pain that continued long after the physical abuse stopped. About the suffering I have in turn caused to loved ones and strangers alike because of what he turned me into.

I estimate that during a ten-year period I was forced to masturbate my dad to orgasm more than 1,500 times.

Numbers on that sort of scale speak for themselves. If you do anything that many times it ceases to be an event. I admit, it soon seemed like pretty mundane behaviour for me.

I was a child, I didn't know any different, so I can't say I was filled with terror on every occasion because it's not true. It was just something that happened. A lot.

It was as much a part of my life as going to school, being made to clean my teeth or squabbling with my sister. It was just another aspect of growing up that I had to get used to.

The biggest crime my father committed, I now realise, was to make me think – make me believe – it was normal. How could I tell the difference? He was my dad. I did what he told me. I didn't like doing it, but there was lots of stuff growing up that I found unpleasant. Eating my greens, as they called it, calling any random adult 'Uncle' or 'Aunty', or helping out around the house – I tried to get out of all of them if I could. As far as I was concerned, masturbating my dad every other day during bath time was just another one of those things that had to be done whether I liked it or not. I never questioned it.

It was just what we did. It's what he taught me.

I never understood many of the events that happened to me as a child, and I use adult language now to describe them. I think that's one reason why the very young who are abused rarely report it. They can't find the vocabulary to express it, nor do they understand it. But they do remember.

I remember.

I realised when I saw him again that day in Lincolnshire that I had been running for too long. For twenty years I thought I could cope on my own and that my only form of defence against this monster was distance. But seeing that poor innocent little kid I realised it was not just about me. There were others going through what I endured. There were other options open to me and I had to take them.

On 16 August 2004 I walked into Grantham police station and reported my own father as a child abuser.

It's over now. Physically at least. The man who robbed me of my innocence is safely behind bars. The nightmares haven't gone away. I don't think they ever will. But I won't let him take another day from me.

My father ruined my childhood but he will not ruin my life. I won't let him. I've turned my fortunes around.

I have a good job, qualifications, a wonderful wife and my

self-respect. There were years when I thought I would never come near to getting any of those. There were years when I thought I would not even make it to this age, because of the paths I was forced down, by the choices I made when I was running from my own past.

But I have made a success of my life.

My name is Duncan Fairhurst. I am an abuse survivor. This is my story.

I

Now It's My Turn

School taught me a lot, and I'm not talking about what was on the national curriculum that particular week. The main lesson is how to fit in. Kids are like sharks. They move in groups and prey on the weak, the young and the different. Pretty much the worst thing you can do at school is stand out. The whole point of the education system isn't about preparing you academically for the grown-up world. It's about training you not to be anything special or different. To not cause a fuss. At least that's how it seemed to me.

And it works. If your mates say they stay up till ten o'clock, eleven o'clock or midnight, then so do you. If they all wear the newest Farah Sta-Pres trousers and brogue shoes, that's what you have to turn up in. It's about being as good as the next bloke. Definitely not any worse, and probably not any better either.

But it's hard. Even Nature seems to conspire against you. For a couple of years every shower after a sports lesson is a nightmare. If you're the first kid to sprout hair under the arms or 'down below', then you're a freak. But if you're the last one to hit puberty, then that's no good either because you're obviously a girl – there must be something wrong with you. The only acceptable thing is to be somewhere in the middle. You have to do everything at the same time as everyone else.

There is a plus side to all this lemming behaviour. Whatever problems you have, you soon learn you're almost certainly not alone. Whatever weird shit is going on in your family, when you're outside the homogenising protection of the school gates, it's comforting to realise something similar is probably going on in a million other families across the country. And that makes all the difference. You can get through anything if your mates are experiencing it too.

At my school, I'd hear all sorts of things. About sex, drugs, you name it. You'd find out about someone's mother being an alcoholic, or a friend's father who got arrested by the police for stealing or maybe for fighting in a bar. Kids used to talk about going out with their dads, having adventures, and being allowed to drive cars or motorbikes. There were some mums who were known for buying their youngsters cigarettes, while a few of my class, the lucky so-and-so's, were allowed to have their girlfriends or boyfriends stay over. Basically, if someone talked about stuff, regardless of how 'out there' it sounded, it made it OK for everyone else.

For example, if you heard someone say, 'I found one of my dad's dirty books, so I had a wank in my bedroom and then I put it back . . .', you knew it was cool to talk about three things: one, wanking; two, dirty books; and three, your dad's dirty books in particular. It sort of set the boundaries and made everything all right.

I learned a lot of things that way. What I never once heard anyone say, however, was 'God, my dad tried to take me up the arse again last night.' And that's when I started to suspect things weren't quite right at my house.

I was born in August 1970 in Kettering in Northamptonshire. I have no memories of living there, for when I was about three or four my family moved to 9 Archers Green, East Goscote. I have a collection of early reminiscences from that address, every one of them vivid although not necessarily in the right order chronologically as I recall them. That's the problem with kids' memories, I suppose. You don't have control over what sticks in your mind. That's another reason so few children or young victims report anything. The police need the sort of dates and facts that the average four- or even ten-year-old can't provide. You just remember what it was like at the time. You don't necessarily remember when that time was in relation to other events. How could you?

It's there, at Archers Green, that I have the first memories of life with my parents and my sister. In my eyes, my father was a superhero. He was immortal, he was strong and, most of all, he was cool. He always answered questions about life, the universe and anything else I threw at him. Better than that, he often cut me a bit of slack – sometimes a lot of slack – where Mum's strict rules and regulations were concerned. I lost track of the number of times he bailed me out by lying about where I was or what I'd been doing when I'd transgressed one of her rules. I loved him for that. I loved him for being Dad.

It's also at Archers Green that I remember mealtimes, playing in the garden, going on day trips and watching television together as a family in the evening. It is at that time that I can picture having fun with my first friends and enjoying my earliest school experiences. Wonderful times – with a few exceptions.

Home was a three-bedroom house with a reasonable sized garden for a child of my age to play in, although I soon outgrew those boundaries. An alley at the bottom of the garden linked all the houses to the main street and my friend Darren Wooley lived at the opposite end to us. If I went to visit him, my mum would telephone his and then each would go down her garden and watch as her son went up or down the alleyway to play with his friend.

I don't think our mothers were actually friends as such, just acquaintances for the sake of their sons being mates. Once when I was playing at the Wooleys' house Mum called to pick me up. As it was summer, Darren's mum, who was called Pat, offered cool refreshments. No sooner had I said, 'Thank you, Pat' than Mother shot me a glance that would sink a battleship. She was good at that. I knew I was in trouble – but why?

As we walked up the alley back to our house Mum launched into the tirade that had been bubbling under for some time. 'How dare you be so rude!' she yelled. 'I've never been so embarrassed. How many times have I told you she is Aunty Pat to you?'

I had no defence. I was guilty as charged. Until I was old enough to ask, 'What should I call you?' I had to suffer the humiliation of calling random adults 'Aunty' or 'Uncle'. It makes me cringe even now to remember it. Sometimes I chose not to speak at all rather than call strangers by these ridiculous titles.

Mum wasn't the only adult to terrify me in that alleyway. Once Darren and I stopped a younger girl from coming up our end of the path. We didn't hurt her or anything, we just blocked the way and called her names. The usual kids' stuff. As far as we were concerned, it was our patch and we didn't want a girl playing there. Later that day when we had to go to Darren's house, we found a man completely blocking the way, just as we had done. It turned out to be the father of the girl from earlier. 'It's not nice, is it?' he said, and refused to let us pass. I can't remember ever feeling quite so scared. If nothing else, it was a valuable lesson: what goes around comes around.

I was intimidated for other reasons by another girl who lived near us. She was called Alison and our mothers were friends, which meant we were often left to play together. Alison's garden had a six-foot fence and a shed, and it was there I remember playing 'you show me yours and I'll show you mine'. It was all so innocent, and we played it a lot with various girls. We were so young that it didn't occur to us that anything else could happen after that.

That was the first time I had ever seen a female other than my sister and mother naked. I had seen my sister Johanna in the bath before but she held no fascination for me. Nor did Mother, but for different reasons. As a young child I found her pubic hair disgusting and I didn't enjoy those occasions when I saw it. It never occurred to me that I would have my own soon enough. At the time it turned my stomach. On the other hand, playing those juvenile games with Alison was mesmerising.

Opposite our house lived a policeman called Tony. He was something of a local celebrity due to his role in the Great Train Robbery – the film, not the heist. Tony was a dog handler and had actually used his own police dog in the scenes directly after the robbery when the police were searching the train and the surrounding area.

He had two dogs, his latest one, Rex, and an Alsatian called Bosun that he had kept after it had finished its stint with the police. I think Bosun must have been a good worker because she had a reputation for not liking anyone except Tony – and me. I don't know what I'd done to win her over, but it came in handy.

Kids in my class were always falling out with their parents, especially after there had been any disciplining incidents, and I was no different. After one particular telling-off I decided, not for the first time, to pack my bags and run away. That would teach them.

I didn't go far. I crossed the road and hid in the dog kennel with Bosun.

It was my father who found me. Unfortunately for him, the dog went berserk when Dad came anywhere near the kennel. In the end he had to wait until Tony came back from helping to look for me. Even then the rescue wasn't over, though, because Bosun wouldn't let Tony approach us either. He had to get his protective handling gear on to chain up the dog and pull me out of there. I think you could say Bosun had a soft spot for me.

Other memories from our days at East Goscote provoke less misty-eyed reminiscence.

It was there that my nightmares started.

Looking back, the content of those dreams seems almost amusing. One vivid episode involved a Womble trying to pull off my nose. There were many like that: ludicrously funny in the cold light of day, but terrifying when you're going through it alone in the darkness. Others were more sinister. The masked assailants, the never-ending corridors, the voices, the constant anxiety – they all became staples of my night-time.

I would often wake up after a nightmare, shaking with fear and unable to get back to sleep. If I cried, Mum would come to see me, sometimes Dad. They both trotted out the usual line, 'It's only a dream.' Then they would close the door and leave me again to my fears.

I dreaded bedtimes and would do my best not to fall asleep in case I had another nightmare. 'Read me a story, Mum, please,' I would cry, desperate to get her to sit with me longer – anything to delay the moment when I'd be left alone with my own scary thoughts. Normally she would stay, but sometimes she would get impatient and just leave me to it.

Some nights I would get out of bed and lie on the landing. If I knelt down I could see the lights from the passing cars through the gap at the bottom of the roller blind in the landing window. For some reason it was hypnotic and comforting. I often fell asleep there. If Mum found me she would pick me up and put me back into bed and I wouldn't even wake.

I still have many of the same nightmares today. As an adult I know they cannot hurt me, however petrifying they seem at the time and however fast my heart beats when I wake, sweating. But I resent the space they take up in my memory. It's always the nasty images that stay with you. The ordinary dreams, the enjoyable ones, have a habit of dispersing like mist before you've even had a chance to savour them.

Sometimes real life is more frightening than the nightmares.

When I was five, I nearly died. I woke up one morning covered in the most perfect fingerprint-shaped bruises. My sister had tickled me the day before, and every movement of her hands to torment me was now recorded on my skin. Five bruises on one thigh, five on each side of my ribs and five on my shoulder. My parents panicked and rushed me to hospital, convinced I had leukaemia.

Their amateur diagnosis turned out to be wrong. That was the good news. The bad news was I did have a disorder called thrombocytopenia which, left unchecked, could very soon lead to haemorrhage, gastrointestinal or even intracranial bleeding. Basically, the doctors explained to me, my blood was lacking in the cells that helped clotting. Bruising was a tell-tale sign. Their only option, they said, was to put me straight into an oxygen tent where I would be quarantined from everyone.

Being at the centre of all this chaos, and seeing the genuine fear in my parents' eyes, was almost unbearable for a five-year-old. No one was allowed to touch me. No one could hug me and make things better.

To make matters worse, it was Christmas. Not only was I trapped inside this stupid tent, but I wasn't even allowed to open any presents in case they were contaminated. The only entertainment I had was the radio. Abba's 'Money Money Money' was in the charts at the time and the BBC played it every hour. I probably never need to hear it again.

My condition really was touch and go at one point, although to hear my mother recount it, you might be forgiven for thinking I had actually died and been reborn. She has always been something of a drama queen, and my illness gave her the perfect opportunity to sponge sympathy off her friends. Many a time during my recuperation I had to listen to the story – my story – being told and retold. 'Black and blue his arms were,' she would say. 'And his skin – you could see right through it!'

To give her her due, Mum was always a great nurse to me. Another time, when I was ill with diarrhoea and confined to the sofa for three days, anything that came out of me, from either end, had to go straight into a bucket – and Mum never flinched from emptying it or cleaning it. And despite all her talk to her friends, she was just as attentive this time when they finally allowed me to go home from hospital.

Long after I was discharged, we still had to return to Leicester Royal Infirmary regularly to have a series of blood tests. Each time the doctor would fill one large syringe and squirt it into two little tubes and then give me an injection. I don't remember what it was. I just know it hurt.

The doctor would then clean the syringes in the sink and give them to me to play with, minus the needles, of course. Over the course of the treatment I built up quite a collection.

The syringes proved a better toy than any water pistol. With practice I found I could squirt water all the way across the back garden or, if I really pumped one up, I could send an arc of liquid above the guttering at the top of the house. A truly amazing feat, I always felt, and a rare happy side-effect of my illness.

Another plus side of being ill was missing school. My entire educational career to date had only totalled a few months, but even so I knew I preferred not being there. By the time I did return to lessons, my infant school was already opening its giant Advent calendar. It was December, and I had been off for almost a year.

On my first morning back, I was allowed the honour of tackling that day's Advent door and, more importantly, eating the bar of chocolate hidden behind it. As the whole school looked on, I pulled back the door and discovered someone had already opened it and stolen the chocolate.

I learned very early on that life was full of disappointments and that the biggest disappointments of all seemed to involve Christmas.

Like most kids, I remember my first inkling that Santa wasn't all he was cracked up to be. My mother likes to tell me it was much later, but this is one of those rare early memories I can put a time and place to. It was the year I went back to school, so it sticks in my memory. I had asked Father Christmas (I wasn't allowed to call him 'Santa') to bring me a wind-up robot for Christmas. I was very specific about this: it had to have red eyes and its chest should open up to reveal flashing laser guns. I remember Mum explaining why she wouldn't buy me a robot while we were out shopping.

'You never know,' she said. 'Father Christmas might bring you one if you are a good boy.'

How many kids fall for that one? I desperately tried to be a good boy, I honestly did, and when Christmas morning came I rushed downstairs to search under the tree for my gifts. I tore open box after box, starting with the ones that looked the right size, but I didn't find my wind-up robot. Ever. What I received instead was a box of Lego which Dad had already opened and had used to erect a poor approximation of said robot. No red eyes and no flashing laser guns. I was gutted. Not only did I not get the one thing I wanted, but I was even denied the pleasure of opening my own Christmas present.

Johanna always seemed to get what she wanted. I remember that year she asked for – and received – a record player. A real one – not a badly constructed plastic version made out of yellow and blue rectangular bricks. She was older than me by four years and so I doubt she would have been content with a set of building blocks, but those little details don't mean much when you're a child. As far as I was concerned at the time, she always got better presents than me because she was Mum's favourite. Since Mum held the purse strings with a vice-like grip, that counted for a lot.

My sister was quite tough on me and I learned the hard way not to trust her. A lot of my mates were picked on by their older siblings, so I never paid much attention to it. That's just the way it was in families, I figured. Although it didn't make the tormenting any easier to deal with at the time.

I once walked into my parents' bedroom and discovered Johanna using Mum's best lipstick to draw all over their new candlewick bedspread. This style was all the rage in those days, and I knew Mum would be livid when she found out – and so did Jo. She flew screaming out of the room as soon as she saw me and told Mum that I had been causing the damage.

I got a serious belting for that.

Jo pulled a similar stunt later, this time by throwing Mum's perfume all over the bed and then blaming me. Yet again my protestations of innocence fell on deaf ears.

With the constant threat hanging over me of being framed for crimes I didn't commit, it felt like my sister could get away with anything if she wanted to.

Even though she knew my problems with nightmares, one of Jo's favourite games was getting me out of bed in the night to tell me stories. If I didn't listen, she threatened to scream and call for Mum – and we both knew what that meant. So whenever Jo felt like it, I would be made to follow her to the bathroom and watch silently while she went to the toilet and made up these ridiculous stories. I don't know what I hated more: being trapped in that tiny room with her or the fact her tales always began with 'A long, long time ago . . .'.

It was not only those times that I felt like a little prisoner in the bathroom. Our mother's habit of watching every penny meant that we cut corners in all sorts of areas, not just with Christmas presents. One of her great attempts at economising was with water. Most houses didn't have proper showers in those days, so to save money we used to only have baths every other day and, when we did, we always shared the water between two. When my sister and I were very young it was not uncommon for us to take a bath together, but after a while we settled into a different routine. My mother would bathe with Jo, and Dad would share with me. I'm sure a lot of families did similar in those days. That's just how it was.

You didn't have to be a member of the family to qualify for the same treatment. As a way of bringing in a few extra pounds, my mum worked from home as a child-minder. She was also a registered foster carer and so our house at Archers Green always had different children running around and sleeping over. None of them stayed very long, but I remember sharing baths with loads of different kids. It was the usual pattern: if they were girls, they shared with Jo, and Mum washed them; the boys came in with me, and Dad saw to us all.

I remember Dad bathing me and a boy called Michael several times. Michael and his sister, Nicola, were with us because their real mum beat them. I never really understood this scenario at the time. I seemed to be smacked every day for stepping out of line somehow or other, and I didn't go to live with anybody else. 'That's not very fair,' I thought.

Once I was actually punished because of Michael. For a joke I locked him out of the house, but after a while he started crying. I was still laughing at him through the window when suddenly my arm was yanked up in the air. I was swung off the ground and my legs were whacked by my irate father.

'Don't you ever do that again, you nasty boy,' he shouted. 'You be nice to your foster brother. Or else.'

All it meant was that I had to be more careful next time.

When I was six my family moved to Dorothy Avenue, Melton Mowbray. Either side of the house lived two ladies, and I was told to call them 'Granny' May and 'Granny' Ruth – I don't know what age you had to be to move up from the fake 'Aunty' title, but they obviously qualified. They were both really nice people. May actually told me I didn't have to call her 'Granny' when Mum was not there, but it had to be our secret because Mum would tell her off if she found out. Both May and Ruth liked to spoil me and my sister from time to time with sweets and chocolate. I was never allowed to spend my pocket money on such luxuries, so they were always welcome treats.

Whether it was down to my mother's penny-pinching or genuine lack of money, I don't know, but we never seemed particularly well off. As a result, my sister and I were taught the value of things at an early age and encouraged to save up our respective pocket money for special occasions. Usually this would translate as Jo having a day out with my mother looking at old country houses and garden centres in the area, while I would be taken swimming by my father. It seemed to be what we each preferred. The 'girls' did one thing, the 'boys' did something else.

I liked those father and son days. I think I was eager for any opportunity to impress my dad and to make him happy with me. Although he rarely spent any time with me at the local baths, Dad would see me safely to the small kiddies' area and then be off doing lengths by himself in the adult pool, showing off how good he was. I used to feel bad that I couldn't swim as well as him. Once he tried to show me how to shallow dive from the edge of the pool, but when it came to my turn I ended up smashing my head into the bottom. Dad comforted me in front of the pool attendants, but I still remember him teasing me as soon as we were in the privacy of the changing room.

We always shared a cubicle to get dressed. Dad would make extra sure my genitals were dry. It didn't matter if I had water on my back, under my arms or if my hair was wringing wet, he always dried my penis and balls quite thoroughly, even when I was capable of doing it by myself.

I never questioned this. It was something else that was 'normal' to me.

Sometimes our trips to the swimming pool coincided with my sister's outing to a local scene of natural beauty. On other occasions just one of us would have their treat and the other would play at home as usual.

For no obvious reason that I can recall, one weekend I suddenly felt an intense need to accompany the 'girls' on that day's trip to a local stately home. It was quite out of the blue. I had no real desire to visit the place – I was more the sporty type, and those stuffy old buildings had no allure for me.

All I do recall is that I did not want to be left at home with Dad.

My mother was having none of it. 'You're just trying to ruin things for your sister, as usual.' I knew she was mistaken, but I could not tell her why. I'm not even sure I understood it myself.

No matter how much I begged, she would not give in. The plans had been made, the packed lunches prepared, and she and Jo were ready to go. 'You're being silly,' she said, as I held on to her coat, crying. 'Now run and play and we'll see you at half past four.'

From the moment the door shut and I watched my mother and sister walk out on to the street, the distinct sense of doom that had been at the back of my mind all day moved to the front. And the worst thing was, I still did not understand the cause.

Despite my apprehension, the rest of the morning came and went and nothing happened. Lunch-time also passed without adventure. Before I realised, it had gone one o'clock and I was still safe from this mysterious impending nightmare. Only a couple more hours until the others were back.

Then, at just after two, my father appeared in the garden where I was playing. 'Come on, Duncan, it's time for a shower.'

This was unusual. Bath time was generally between six and eight, depending on whether it was a school night or not. But Father knew best.

When I went into the bathroom, Dad was already there. As usual I took my clothes off and he undressed himself. We didn't have a separate shower as such. A little rubber hose with a shower-head on it was connected to both bath taps, and sometimes I would sit underneath the jet of water while Dad washed me.

On this occasion, I had to wait for my shower.

'Lie on the floor, Duncan, there's a good lad.'

Confused, I did as I was told and lay naked on the strip of carpet alongside the bath.

'Dad, what are you doing?'

'Quiet, son,' he said. 'You'll enjoy this.'

I'm sure my father must have noticed the nervousness in my voice, but that didn't stop him from rubbing my penis with his hands and, when I got an erection, from putting it inside his mouth to give me oral sex.

Up and down his mouth went while I lay there motionless. It seemed to go on for ever and I did not ejaculate. I was too young. Soon it began to hurt.

'Daddy,' I said. 'I'm sore.'

He stopped and lay down beside me.

'Now,' he said, 'it's my turn.'

The words are as clear in my memory – and as terrifying – now as they were then. 'What's going on?' I thought. 'What does "my turn" mean? What does he want me to do?'

I didn't have to wait long to find out.

The worst, however, was yet to come. I didn't appreciate at the time that what my father had just done to me, and what he wanted me to do next, would not be a one-off. The things I remember being subjected to that day were to become a regular part of my everyday life for the next eight years.

This was just the beginning.

2

You Do Love Daddy, Don't You?

I never knew my grandparents. Mum's father, a policeman called Edward Ford, died when I was six months old. The others had passed away before I was born. Everything I know about them I've heard from my parents. My middle names are 'Edward Charles', after my grandfathers.

Mum lost her mother when she was five. As she tells it, her father was then pressured into remarrying as quickly as possible in order to protect his job. In those days, the idea of a single father raising a small child and holding down a post on the Lincoln police force was unthinkable. There was no state help and, what's more, I don't think being a single parent was the done thing, whatever the circumstances. So he married Muriel.

Or 'the Wicked Witch of the West' as my mother still calls her. According to Mum, she showed favouritism towards her own child, Mum's stepsister Elizabeth.

Elizabeth, apparently, was showered with love and devotion from Muriel while Mum received a cold shoulder at the best of times, and absolute contempt for the rest. If there were treats, Elizabeth got them. The only special treatment Mum received was being sent to boarding school as soon as she was old enough. Elizabeth was educated locally.

Mum hated being so far from home and ran away several times. On each occasion she was found and taken back to the school. Then one day, when she was ten, her father arrived to pick her up and said she didn't have to go back any more if she didn't want to.

To hear Mum talk about him, Edward Ford was the original candidate for World's Best Dad. I think that's why she liked Tony opposite so much. All coppers remind her of her father.

I know how she felt. That's how I felt about my own dad. He was the greatest man on Earth. He was immortal in my eyes.

Mum went to nursing college in Leicester when she was sixteen. After a two-year foundation course and three years' training she became a nurse. Nearly ten years later, when she was working as a district nurse, she met my dad. He used to say he married her because she looked good in her nurse's uniform and she had a car. She said 'yes' because she was over thirty and didn't want to be left on the shelf. She wanted children.

I don't think love entered into it.

Or sex. According to Mum, there was no kissing or any other sexual contact before the wedding night. For her, the reasons for abstaining were 'religious'. Like a lot of women of her generation, she was raised to see sex before marriage as 'un-Christian'. More important, it would also earn you an undesirable 'reputation' among your peers which, for my mother, was worse than any biblical edict.

My father's grounds for abstention are not so clear.

When the moment came, it was not memorable. Mum later confided to me that Dad apparently knew nothing about a woman's 'bits', as she called them. Or, if he did know, he did not care. Their wedding night involved no foreplay. Dad hopped on and rolled off when he was done.

It seemed that my parents' sex life remained very limited, to Mum's regret. 'Sex is for making babies,' Dad had explained early in their marriage.

Mind you, it worked. My sister, Jo, was a product of their honeymoon. Mum later had two miscarriages. Then I came along.

I never saw my parents kiss, except for a peck on the cheek when, for example, they exchanged gifts at Christmas. I never saw them hold hands. They never cuddled or showed any affection towards each other at all. I remember there was a time while we were at Melton when I began to see them more as partners in a house and family than as partners in love. They were businesslike in their approach to each other and to us kids. They shared money and responsibilities and co-owned a property. They did what they had to do. Nothing more.

They were two very different peas who just happened to live in the same pod.

Mum often said Dad was 'the best of a bad bunch – his whole family are crooks'.

My great-grandfather on my dad's side was an Irishman from a travelling fair. Dad was the middle of seven children, with thirty years separating first and last. In descending order they were: Charley, Ken, Pearl, Clifford (Dad), Len, Pat and Joyce.

Charley and Ken both fought in the Second World War. One was shot in the backside; the other was a sailor whose ship went down but who survived. Both spent time in prison after the war and are now dead.

The family lived in a council house on the Braunston Estate in Leicester. Dad's parents died within weeks of each other while he was the eldest child still living at home. The council said they could keep the tenancy on the house if Dad looked after his younger three siblings. If he declined, they would be taken into care.

He might as well have said 'no' for all the good it did. Len moved out to live with Christine, who would soon be his wife. Pat ran away from home and had a reputation as a bit of a handful by the age of fifteen. Joyce emigrated to Australia at the earliest opportunity and subsequently has little to do with anyone from the family. I think I met her once but don't know her at all.

No one stayed with my father for a moment longer than they had to.

According to Mum, Dad's family believed a woman's place is in the kitchen – or in bed. It did not help that they were also strict Catholics, at least when it came to contraception. Charley had eleven children. Kenneth had fourteen.

Dad, on the other hand, reckoned the Fairhursts were like the Royal Family of the council estates in Leicester. As far as he was concerned, they were loyal and normal and loving, and they all looked up to him as being successful in business. For some reason they all called him 'our John' rather than Clifford. John is his middle name.

When we lived in East Goscote, we would often drive over to Leicester to visit one or other of Dad's siblings. Normally on the way back we'd drop in on Aunty Pat and Uncle Dave. She was Dad's favourite: it was always 'relative plus Pat' on our days out.

She had three boys, Christopher, Kevin and Raymond.

Raymond was the same age as me, Christopher and Kevin were three years older. When I was very young we all played together in their garden or out in the street in front of the house. Chris and Kevin were charged with my care. They were 'big boys' according to the adults.

I loved Aunty Pat and Uncle Dave. I thought they were much nicer than my parents, and their kids seemed to have a better time than my sister and I did. My cousins had much more personal freedom than we could ever hope to have.

When I came out of the hospital after having thrombocytopenia, I was sent to stay with Aunty Pat and Uncle Dave for a weekend. This was to allow Mum and Dad to spoil my sister, as I had been the centre of attention for so long. It was meant to be a treat for her, but I think I was just as happy, if not more so, to actually be 'living' with my favourite relatives.

When we moved to Melton Mowbray, things changed. As it was further away we couldn't so easily pop over, and gradually the regular visits dried up. Wherever we lived, they never came to us. We were always the ones who made the effort. I don't think they could drive. Sometimes Pat came along when one of her other brothers drove over, but we never had the whole family to stay.

We used to see Mum's cousin Robert quite a lot, and once he brought his wife Cathy and family to visit. He had two daughters, one my age and one a year older than Johanna, and the four of us spent the afternoon locked up in my room, with the trapdoor locked down to keep out nosy adults. Someone came up with the idea of playing 'doctors and nurses', and since I was the only boy, I automatically became the patient. At some point, the eldest 'doctor' showed me her breasts as part of the game. I don't remember if I had to show her anything in return.

Mum always sang the praises of Robert and Cathy, but after a while I realised we had not seen them for ages. When I asked Mum about it she dismissed my question. 'Don't be silly, Duncan, we see them all the time.' But we didn't. Not from that point on. They retired to France and never even said goodbye.

I guess pretending to be nurses was logical for us, considering Mum's background. She was still a professional working woman when she got married. She told me much later that Dad beat her up badly soon after they moved in together. He wanted 'to put her in her place', show her who was boss in their relationship. I never saw it, but he beat her a couple of times over the years. Sometimes it only needs one beating to subdue a person.

They argued a lot. About everything; the more trivial the better. It made me feel bad to hear the shouting, things being thrown, plates smashed, doors slamming. But that was how they lived. That was how we all lived.

They always argued at the dinner table. The same subjects set them off each time. Dad using the 'wrong' wooden spoon (we had one for stirring baked beans, one for stirring stew . . .) was a favourite. Or Mum not calling Dad in from outside before dinner was ready, leading to him moaning that by the time he'd washed his hands his food was cold.

Mum always pleaded poverty but we seemed to eat well. By that I mean we had reasonably healthy food, and we certainly never went hungry. We only had fried food once a week, and that was for lunch on Saturday.

Dad was a good cook. He did his national service in the

RAF and was a chef in the officers' mess. He cooked great fry-ups.

Mum was also a good cook, but she always seemed stressed by the effort. I dreaded her Sunday lunches. The food was good, but she always scolded us for transgressing some unwritten rule of etiquette, for not being quick enough to pass something or for doing something else before she was ready. It was almost as if she resented us for not understanding telepathically what she wanted us to do.

Sunday lunch was an obligatory family time. We were supposed to make small talk and chat about things we had done or were going to do. It always felt strained. What usually happened was that Mum talked at us while we ate. We were never allowed to leave the table until everyone had finished, and she was always last.

I wasn't allowed to refuse to eat anything. I hated Brussels sprouts. I couldn't stomach them then and I still can't today. But Mum insisted on serving them up. I always tried to eat them to please her, but on more than one occasion they made me gag. Occasionally I even vomited.

The only time my parents seemed to get on was when we had visitors, or we were 'out'. They were different then, changing into model parents. As soon as whoever it was left, they would revert back into bickering, arguing, normal Mum and Dad.

Visitors were few and far between, though, just the odd family member. Neither Mum nor Dad ever had friends over to the house. They never threw dinner parties or went out to dinner with other couples. Occasionally, out of absolute necessity, they would go to a works function, but even that stopped when Dad went self-employed.

They were not shy – I remember once, when we were out shopping, Mum lectured a young mother, 'You should take more care of that baby' – or incapable of being friendly. She would chat to a woman who served her in a shop or the person on the till in the supermarket. But that's where it ended.

The arguing would have been worse if Dad had been around more. He had his family time and his personal time. He was rarely there except at designated 'off-duty' times. Anything to do with the family was Mum's responsibility. If we were sick, he didn't hang around to help. He often 'worked late' or went out somewhere.

Mum never questioned him about where he was going. She didn't dare.

The only household responsibility Dad took without complaint was for bath times.

No kid I knew enjoyed having to wash. It's as if all young boys are born with a highly developed soap allergy. Unless you're going to pee, bathrooms are places to be avoided.

I was a typical lad in that respect. Unless I was in a swimming pool, I hated getting wet. Events on the afternoon when my father said, 'Now it's my turn' only intensified that feeling. I couldn't shake off the sensation of horror I felt all that day. I couldn't forget any of the detail of what happened subsequently. Most of all, I couldn't understand any of it. I had never felt so confused.

When my sister and mother returned from their visit to the stately home that Saturday, they had no idea that anything was different – or wrong. Despite my deep unease, I had no idea that anything was actually wrong either. Kids have short attention spans and remarkable powers of recovery. A spanked child returns for cuddles within half an hour.

I did not like what happened in the bathroom, certainly, but that did not make it bad. My dad was very clear about this. Some things you have to do because they're right or they're good for you. Like eating your greens.

I did feel different when I left the bathroom that afternoon, though. By the time I walked past the lounge, Dad was asleep on the sofa. That was normal. If anything was wrong, he wouldn't be able to sleep, would he? I went in the garden to play. I could always lose myself in that garden. There was an apple tree to climb, there was a shed behind which I could build dens. What happened in the house seemed a world away.

Two days later and I was due another bath. This was a school night, so it was in the evening, just before I went to bed. Throughout the day I had a sense of impending doom in the back of my mind, just like before. As the afternoon wore on it became more prominent. It felt as if I was going to get spanked, as though Mum had said, 'You wait till your father gets home . . .', but I knew I hadn't done anything wrong.

Dinner that evening was even harder to eat. Mum and Dad bickered as normal. I played with my food, pushing it around my plate rather than putting it in my mouth. No one would leave the table if I hadn't finished. That was the rule.

As usual Dad took me to the bathroom. I didn't understand what had happened the time before, but I knew I didn't like it. It wouldn't happen again, would it?

If I told Dad I didn't like it, that would be all right, wouldn't it?

When he came into the bathroom and locked the door behind him, I was still fully clothed. 'Come on, lad, take your things off. You can't have a bath all dressed like that.'

I was almost breathless with relief. I was just having a bath after all. As normal. Quickly, before Dad changed his mind, I removed my socks and shorts, took off my short-sleeved shirt and began to pull down my pants. Then I noticed. Leaning against the bathroom door, Dad was pulling one leg out of his own trousers. He was taking his clothes off.

It was going to happen again.

I started to shiver and told Dad I wasn't happy. He smiled. 'Come on, Duncan, don't be silly,' he said. 'You're going to give your daddy a flick.' 'Flick' was his word for what I did to him. I never heard anyone else use it.

'This is what daddies and their little boys do to show they love each other.'

As before, he sat on the floor and made me sit next to him. Then he put a hand on my shoulder and eased me back, so I was lying down next to him. Leaning over me, he stroked my penis with his forefinger, then started to roll it between his finger and thumb.

I was terrified. I shut my eyes and tried not to think about what was happening to me.

'Relax, Duncan,' Dad said. 'Just enjoy it.'

I was scared. I didn't know why we were doing this. I didn't like what it did to me. Things were beginning to happen to my body without my control. My little penis in my dad's fingers was starting to grow. I watched as it stiffened and doubled in size. Dad seemed happy with this. He smiled as he stroked. His touch got harder, he started to pinch, he was rough and it began to hurt. I felt different in my tummy, as if I was nervous or excited. I knew it had something to do with what was being done to me, but I did not know how or why.

'Daddy,' I said eventually, 'it hurts. I don't like it. Please stop.' He looked at me and seemed to nod.

Given what happened next, I wish he had carried on touching me.

Dad made me sit up again and this time he rested his head on the floor. 'Give me your hand,' he said, and he placed it over his lap. I tried to resist but he forced my fingers down so I was pressing into the flesh of his penis. He was already hard and I could see it was pointing up his stomach towards his belly button. My hand brushed against the hair from his testicles and his groin. I was scared. It was so different from my own body.

I called my penis my 'wee wee'. That was Mum's word for it. Penises were dirty things, for using to go to the toilet. For that reason alone I knew it was wrong to touch Dad's wee wee. All I could think about was the germs that Mum said we would catch if we weren't clean.

But Dad wasn't thinking about hygiene. He put both my hands around his penis and clamped his own hand on top. 'Look,' he said, 'watch me. Do what I'm doing.'

Slowly he brought our hands up and then down. Again and again. I didn't understand what we were doing, but I knew it was the same thing he did to me. I didn't enjoy it. Why would he? Then he took his own hand away and rested back as I was left to do it on my own.

It didn't take long before my arms started to ache. 'I'm tired, Daddy,' I said, but he made me continue.

I couldn't understand. Why wouldn't he let me stop? I could see in his face I was hurting him. His eyes were screwed shut and he was clenching his teeth as if he was trying to ignore the pain. Why did he want me to hurt him? Was it because he hurt me? Did he want to punish himself because of it? My feelings didn't matter now. I just didn't want him to be hurt any more.

After a few minutes, he suddenly said, 'That's enough,' and, taking my hands away, he rolled on to his side, vigorously rubbing himself up and down as he'd shown me.

For a moment I felt sad, thinking that I'd done something wrong. I had disappointed him and he had to do it himself. My sorrow soon turned to something else.

With his spare hand Dad grabbed a piece of toilet paper to put on the floor between us. I watched, by turns fascinated and repulsed, as he seemed to be hurting his own penis. His face became contorted in pain, reddening with each hand movement. His penis looked sore, almost bruised. What had I done to it? Had I broken it?

And then it got worse.

It was just like before. White stuff came spurting out of his wee wee and on to the tissue paper. Some missed. I watched as it landed on the bathroom carpet. Dad was sweating now. He didn't seem to be noticing anything. His hand was wet, he was mumbling to himself, and then he looked down at his penis and squeezed it really hard over the tissue.

I felt sick.

Why was he hurting himself like this? Was it my fault? The end of his penis looked swollen and purple. Small, white droplets trickled out and dripped on to the tissue and the carpet. Why didn't he let go? Why didn't he make the nasty swelling stop?

So many thoughts were going through my mind that I had forgotten what he had done to me. Why was his penis leaking like this? What was this white liquid? Why didn't Dad do whatever it was in the toilet?

My penis had never hurt me like this. Was it a type of blood? Had I injured him?

I was shocked. Numbed, I think, by what I saw. The mess was disgusting. The look on Dad's face was too disturbing to imagine. What, would happen next?

No sooner had I thought it than Dad pulled himself up and clambered to his feet. With me just feet away he stood over the toilet and started to urinate. 'You've got to clean the pipes,' he said.

I did not know what he meant.

Dad didn't talk about what had just happened. It was exactly like last time.

After he had cleaned himself and flushed the toilet, he diverted his attention back to me. He ran the bath until there was about six inches of water in it, then I climbed in and he hosed me down with the rubber shower attachment that clipped to the taps.

He was very attentive. He wanted to make sure I was OK, that the water was the right temperature, that I was happy. By Dad's standards I was being pampered.

And then he started to talk about earlier.

'You do love Daddy, don't you?'

I nodded. Of course I did. What a question. I loved my mum, I loved my sister and I loved my dad. He took me fishing, he took me for walks in the country, we played together in the garden. Everyone loves their dad. We were a normal family. Of course I loved mine.

As he spoke to me, Dad stroked my hair as if he was patting a pet dog.

I told him I didn't like what had just happened. He explained again that it's what people who love each other do. 'Everyone who loves their children does this,' he said. 'And I will always love you.'

I must have said something else then – I can't remember exactly what – because he told me that even though everyone does it, people pretend they don't.

'It's like speeding, Duncan,' he explained. 'The law says it's wrong but everyone does it. You're too young to understand.'

All I had to know, he said, was if people found out about the way we loved each other, Daddy would be sent to prison. That would be unfair because the policeman who took Daddy away, even the judge who sent Daddy to prison, would all love their little boys in the same way.

'You don't want Daddy to be sent to prison, do you?'

No. No no no. Now I was really scared. I couldn't imagine life without him.

He made me promise not to tell anyone else about how we loved each other. I agreed.

'Good lad,' he said and ruffled my hair again. 'It's between you and me. Our little secret.'

3

Something New to Worry About

My parents were snobs. They looked down on all tradesmen, people like road sweepers, cleaners or dustmen. In Leicester, our nearest city, there is a phenomenon called 'July fortnight'. This is the first two weeks of the school summer holidays when all the local council estates decamp and head off to the seaside to Skegness. We never, ever went away during this period.

We used to go on holiday every August to a place called Trusthorpe. It was a nice enough seaside town on the Lincolnshire coast between Sutton on Sea and Mablethorpe. It was all right, nothing special. But the main thing it had going for it was that it wasn't Skegness.

In Skegness for those two weeks when the July fortnighters were there, crime rates soared, shops' takings increased and drinking and fights went through the roof. Obviously, both the place and the people who frequented it were too tacky for the Fairhursts. Even Mablethorpe, in my parents' eyes, wasn't good enough for us, although we occasionally went there for the odd spot of shopping, or in the evening we might stroll over so my parents could have a drink in the beach bar that was a café during the day and served alcohol at night. Mum's drink was always Dubonnet and lemonade; Dad's was lager.

It's hard to feel superior when your holiday home is a static caravan, but somehow my parents managed it. For two weeks every year, from when we lived at East Goscote till we left Melton, we stayed in the same one: white with a blue stripe around the middle.

One day, while making dinner in the caravan, Mum spilt chicken soup into my lap. I screamed and screamed and screamed. It was agony. Dad picked me up, ripped off my jeans and pants and stuck me under the cold tap. We went to the local cottage hospital and I was given some cream. It was not exactly life-threatening but it really hurt. Pain stays in the memory long after the good times have faded.

Another hangover from our East Goscote days was our cat. My mum always gave our pets daft names, and this was no exception. Yowlee was a chocolate Siamese with brown markings. He was an excellent pet – cuddly and apparently willing to be mauled by children. He came on holiday with us, but the best thing about Yowlee, was that he used to like to go on walks with us. We would stroll from Trusthorpe to the Mablethorpe beach bar with him trotting along the sea wall on a long extending lead next to us. If there was a gap in the brickwork that he couldn't leap across, like steps to the beach or the slipway, he would hop on to Dad's or Mum's shoulder until he could jump down on to the sea wall again.

We always sat outside the bar and Yowlee would curl up around Dad's neck like a muffler and go to sleep. That raised a few eyebrows from the passing holidaymakers. 'Is he dead?' people would say, or 'Is it real?' Yowlee didn't seem to care about spots of rain or wind, he just liked going for walks.

We were a big pets household. There were always cats around the place, wherever we lived. They always liked to sit on top of the boiler when it was warm. At one stage we had five cats, three dogs and dozens of gerbils and a hamster. The names were all down to my mother: Yowlee, Malcheck, Bertie, Smudge and Tabatha were all cats. Then there were the dogs – Stranger was an alsatian, Brandy was a dachshund and Carlos was our tiny chihuahua. It wasn't all plain sailing with so many animals. I remember Mum raging because Tabatha had urinated in one of her precious Christmas cactus plants and killed it. I liked them around the house. They were all friendly and I enjoyed their company.

One of the things my parents always argued about was money. Dad liked to think of himself as a bit of a wheeler-dealer. We never saw any evidence of it. Mum says she couldn't trust him with money. If she gave him a tenner to buy some bread she would naturally kiss goodbye to any hope of seeing some change. In that way, he was 'tight'. But whenever we ate out, Dad always paid. That was the man's job.

Our caravan in Trusthorpe had a toilet but no shower. Both of these proved troublesome in their own way. We were not allowed to go for a 'number two', as my mum called it, in the caravan, only a 'number one', and even that only at night. During the day we had to go to the shower blocks and use the toilets there.

The facilities were not exactly state of the art, but they worked. The showers were very old-fashioned, with concrete floors and walls and wooden doors. All the years we went there, Dad and I always showered in the same cubicle. I never questioned it. It was just what we did.

I was very young when Dad made me masturbate him in the shower there.

'Will you wash me, Duncan?' he asked.

I looked up at him for a second. Then I realised what he meant. He didn't say 'flick', which was his normal code, but it was clear what he wanted.

'Come on, soap up.' I did as I was told. I rubbed the bar of soap between my hands until I had a decent lather. Then I reached out for his penis and started to 'wash' it.

I don't remember how long it took that time. I don't remember what he said, or what he made me do. All I remember is him ejaculating. I can still see his sperm splattered on the floor as the shower water started to wash it down the drain.

The next thing I remember is running to get away from the toilet blocks as fast as possible. In my hurry I fell and cut my hand on broken glass. As I struggled to get up, I saw the blood pouring from my palm.

Dad was first on the scene. He took me back to our caravan where Mum had a look and pronounced that I needed stitches. I carry that scar on my hand to this day.

One of my mother's other rules on those holidays was that we weren't allowed to buy 'tat'. We had a bucket and spade and that was it. Once I wanted to buy a wooden plane with a propeller that was powered by an elastic band. Mum wouldn't let me; she said it was junk and I would break it within ten minutes. We were never allowed to spend our pocket money on what we liked. We could buy sweets, but only so many each day.

They even decided who I could talk to. When I was six I was told off for talking to an orthodox Jewish family, for some reason. I remember being fascinated by the tassels they had at the side of their head. They were friendly enough but I wasn't allowed to play with them.

On the way home, every year without fail, we had to sing daft songs in the car. I hated singing. I still do.

The singing was not the only regular occurrence of our holidays. 'Soaping up' in the shower proved to be more than a one-off. On every visit there were one or two occasions. They stick in my mind because my father never said 'give me a flick', as he did at home.

Even when I didn't have to touch him, Dad still made us shower together. I don't remember how many stalls there were, but there was always at least one other empty cubicle when we went in there.

They were all empty whenever Dad made me wash him like that.

When we first moved to Melton I went to an infant school for a term, then moved up to the Grove County Primary School. It had a wide catchment area and there were a fair few kids on the register so it was pretty big. Once we had a police car driver come to give a talk to our class. The playground was so large that he was able to drive his car around with his siren blaring and lights flashing while we watched.

It was at Grove that I made some good friends: Anthony, Paul and another Darren.

Anthony Burke and his sister Miranda lived on the same side of Dorothy Avenue as us, but a bit further up. Paul Jaggard lived at the top of the street, and Darren Townsend lived more or less opposite our house.

Paul had an older, disabled brother. He was the first person

I ever saw in a wheelchair. I didn't go to Paul's house much as it was too far. Actually, it was only a few hundred yards away, but because it was out of sight it was out of bounds. Maybe Mum didn't like the Jaggards. I was allowed to go out of sight to the bottom of the street to buy her cigarettes, but I wasn't allowed to go the same distance in the other direction to play with my friend.

I bought the cigarettes from a corner shop run by a Sikh family called the Singhs. The daughter was at Grove with me and we were friends. This made me quite unusual. Most of my other friends hated Asians because they were 'different'. One day Mum said I could play at Darren's with my friends if, on my way back, I picked up a newspaper she had ordered. As usual, instead of staying at Darren's we slipped off to play on some railway tracks at an abandoned yard some distance away. It was a great place to walk dogs or pick blackberries in the autumn, but Mum would never have allowed me to go there if she had known. On the way back I found the ten pence in my pocket that Mum had given me for the newspaper. My friends laughed at me for going to the Singhs. They said the shop smelled 'funny' (none of us had ever eaten curry) and that 'brown people' were dangerous because they were not like us.

In the end I bought the paper from a different shop. That was hardly the crime of the century, but I forgot that Mr Singh had put a copy of the paper aside for Mum. A couple of days later, when she went over to the shop, she was asked why she hadn't picked it up. Mum was adamant that I had already been over and paid for it.

Back home, though, with no strangers watching, it was a different story. 'Why didn't you buy my newspaper from the

Singhs?' Mum raged. 'Why did you lie to me about where you bought it? Why did you lie?' It was only over a cheap newspaper, but I was terrified. In the end I confessed everything, about playing with my friends and finding a 'white' newsagent.

The funny thing is, Mum never said anything about the racist stuff. I had lied to her and she had lied to Mr Singh. Still in a fury, she marched me down the road to the shop and made me apologise to him while she glared down. I think Mr Singh was used to this kind of thing, but his daughter never spoke to me again.

Mum's rules were hard to follow sometimes. I was often 'grounded' and banned from leaving the house, although I never really considered it a punishment as we had such a large garden. It was as long and as wide as the house. Half consisted of grass and borders, the other half was given over to vegetables and fruit bushes, like loganberries, blackberries and gooseberries. At the bottom was a big apple tree, great for climbing, and to the right of that was a shed. I was always happy playing out there. If Mum had been smarter, the next time I was late home from school or I didn't quite finish my greens, she would have banned me from the garden rather than sending me out there. The only downside was that I spent a lot of time alone. Johanna was never grounded, but she never went anywhere without Mum anyway.

My form tutor at Grove was Miss Prazlik. We took the mickey out of her behind her back, because she had a pronounced limp when she walked. Another example of someone out of the ordinary . . .

I was in her class on the top floor when Mrs Thatcher banned free milk in schools. One day we had it at break times and the next we didn't. I never liked it anyway, as it was always warm, but lots of people were very angry about it.

Another highlight of her class was the arrival of Matthew the Australian. He very quickly became the coolest kid in the school because he was so sporty. He had a football on a rope which we all laughed at at first, but once we saw how many 'keepy uppies' he could do with it, everyone was soon walking around with one.

Except me. Footballs attached to the end of rope were filed under 'waste of money' in my mother's mind, along with most other kids' fads. It is very hard to fit in when you don't have the same toys as everyone else.

Mum thought it was better to try to support me in other ways. She insisted on taking part in school sports days, much to my embarrassment. Once I came second in the three-legged race, and at senior school I somehow fluked first in the shot putt, but generally I was a middle-of-the-field athlete, not at the front and not at the back. My mum, though, always came last. That meant people noticed her. And that meant they noticed me. I know she meant well, but I wish she hadn't bothered.

The local cub scout group was held at Grove on weekday evenings, so it wasn't too far to go if I wanted to join. The hut was at the bottom of the playground, and parents had to drive through the school to drop their sons off. Dad was very keen, so I was signed up for the six-week trial. Some of the boys there needed longer arms to fit all their badges on, but I only managed to pass one for sport. When the time came for my investiture, though, things did not go according to plan. As a seven-year-old I felt foolish having to swear an oath to God and the Queen, and I wouldn't do it. No oath, no membership. I think I was probably the first cub to be ejected for conscientious objection.

Dad was annoyed with me for being thrown out. He had ties to the group and used to be leader of his own troop in Leicester. He had stayed in touch with another leader from that group and they used to go on weekend camping trips together to a place called Johns Lee Woods.

Sometimes when we lived in Melton we would go on day trips as a family. One of my favourites was a visit to Warwick Castle. It was a long drive away so we had to get up early. The fact that I was so excited by images of knights and battles and suits of armour meant that the journey seemed to take even longer.

The castle itself was everything I had hoped for from watching films about days of yore. I pictured myself living there among the old paintings, the tapestries and ancient wooden furniture, drinking from silver goblets and having jousting competitions to win a fair maiden's hand. The two towers in the main castle walls both had spiral staircases which seemed to go on for ever when we were climbing up. It was great fun.

The only disappointment that day was the fact that it was so busy. It was during the summer holidays, so it was warm enough to have a picnic on the grass inside the castle, but there were people swarming everywhere around 'my' home.

We looked around the main part of the castle as a family in the morning, then in the afternoon we split up. Mum and Johanna went to the gift shop, while Dad and I went to the dungeons. I had never seen anything like the array of torture equipment they had down there. I was fascinated by the Iron Maiden coffin – imagine being shut in there with all its spikes skewering through you! Then there was a metal frame you got hung up in until you died, and a tiny room called a 'forgettery' or oubliette, which was a hole in the ground with an iron grid hatch in which people were imprisoned and forgotten about until they starved to death.

Every deadly implement from that trip sticks in my memory today, but the thing I remember most is that my dad took so many pictures of me down there in the dungeons – literally dozens of photographs of me by this grisly machine or up against that wall. All I wanted to do was carry on exploring, but Dad just kept snapping away. 'Look this way,' he said. Then, 'Look up at that light.' He didn't seem to notice how embarrassed I was or how awkward I looked. It didn't help that the dungeons were so busy. People kept walking between us and he got more and more annoyed. I could feel myself turning red as he positioned me this way and that, oblivious to the numerous onlookers waiting to get past. If they got in his way he just told them to move.

As usual we had a sing-song in the car on the way home. This time it was songs from *Mary Poppins* and *The Sound of Music*. I hated it, but Dad often said I had a really good voice and should be a choirboy.

Our home in Melton was a spacious bungalow in a terrace. The bottom half of Dorothy Avenue consisted of bungalows and the top half of houses. Our place was the second to last bungalow before the houses started. The property was set about two metres back from the road, separated from the pavement by a small brick wall. As you went in through the blue front door, on the right was the biggest room, the living-room. On the left was my sister's room, followed by Mum and Dad's room. Straight ahead was the bathroom. I can barely think of it without shivering.

The hall turned to the right into the dining-room and left into the kitchen. A hatch in the wall between them meant Mum could pass food through into the dining-room area. The back door from the kitchen to the garden was like a stable door. You could open the top half and lock the bottom.

I remember Mum holding me on her hip looking out the door at a dry thunderstorm. We watched the lightning but there was no rain. She explained that there might be a fire somewhere because there was no rain to put out the fire that lightning made.

Tucked under the work surface in the kitchen was a twin-tub washing machine that Mum used to pull out to use. It was fascinating to watch. You could open the lid and look inside and watch the clothes go round and round. It sounds silly now to have gained pleasure from such mundane things.

Leaning against the hall wall next to the living-room door was a big, black, wooden stepladder. If you pulled it out to the appropriate angle you could go up and push aside a hatch leading to the attic, which had been converted into an extra room. That was my bedroom.

Compared with my box room at East Goscote, this was a palace. By any standards the room was massive, pretty much taking up 80 per cent of the entire bungalow's loft space. Below were the living-room, bathroom and the other two bedrooms.

Being on a different floor I felt like I was in my own little world. I could retreat upstairs and feel safe. If I pulled the hatch over, I could pile books and toys on top of it and then no one could get in. I was king of the castle.

Two small doors led to a strange area in the eaves which was used for storage. I built a den using the stuff I found in there. It added another level of security where I could read my comics unbothered.

For a six-year-old, using a stepladder to get to my room was like having a little adventure every time. I loved it. Mum didn't feel the same. Without a proper staircase she was never comfortable climbing up into the attic, and so she hardly ever came into my room.

This meant that Dad normally tucked me into bed.

I enjoyed the times when I was alone with my father. Sharing anything when you're a kid seems unnatural. Being told by Mum something as normal as 'Let your sister have some of your sweets' seemed a personal affront, even if Johanna had to reciprocate at other times. Sharing Dad with the rest of the family was no different, which is why I cherished the times when I had him to myself.

Even the bath times. Although I didn't like the routine we had settled into every other night – I hated the things we did each time, and what he made me do – I knew it was his way of showing he loved me.

Bedtimes were different. I looked forward to hearing my father's steps as he climbed the ladder. That was my cue to hop into bed. By the time his head appeared through the entrance in the floor, I was always safely under the covers, ready to be kissed goodnight. Normally Dad would sit next to me and we would chat about what I'd been doing that day. I can't remember the specific conversations now, but I recall being happy when they took place. It was 'us' time, just me and Dad, and nobody was going to tell me to share him.

One night he knelt next to my bed, as usual, and pulled back the blankets.

'Take down your pyjamas,' he said. Lifting my bottom in the air, I shunted along the bed until I was able to tug my trousers around my ankles. 'That will do,' Dad said. It was not a bath night so I did not feel worried. But I was confused.

Seconds later everything became clear. Dad picked up my exposed penis and started to stroke. He was gentle, caressing as you would someone's hand. He was staring intently as he worked, oblivious to the petrified face inches away from his.

I was desperate not to get an erection. I couldn't forget the agony he appeared to be in when I touched his penis in the bathroom. I didn't want to suffer in the same way he did.

And I certainly did not want any white stuff to come out of me.

Dad didn't seem to mind that I didn't 'change'. He was quite casual in his motions, just enjoying the sensation and watching. Then, as quickly as he'd started, he stopped. 'Come on then, time for sleep.' I pulled my pyjamas up as quickly as I could and dragged the blankets over me tightly. Dad kissed me on the head and said goodnight. As he descended the step-ladder I started to shiver.

Now I had something new to worry about.

4

The World's Strongest Man

All of my friends used to tell me, 'Your dad's cool, Duncan.' That made me proud. The best thing was, I thought so too.

Within the four walls of our house Johanna and I were under Mum's jurisdiction, but at weekends or during holidays, Dad would take us out, and that was when the fun started.

We often went on walks in the countryside. One of our favourite spots was a village called Syston. We would park the car in a lay-by and clamber up a stile to get over the hedge. Compared to my height at the time, it was a huge obstacle to climb over but what lay the other side made it worth it.

Inside a big field (giant from a youngster's point of view) was a picture-postcard brook that burbled down the right-hand side of the hedge. I stood on the bank with Dad and fished with a green net on a long bamboo stick. We collected frogspawn and caught the odd stickleback, which we put in jars to take home. It was quite idyllic.

In autumn I would collect conkers from the horse chestnut tree in the middle of the field.

Anything dangerous like playing with the conkers back home, however, came back under Mum's remit. Collecting them was fine, even climbing up into the trees to knock them down was allowed. But I wasn't permitted to put a string through them and hit anyone else's until I was much older. I was certainly never allowed to bake them in vinegar like the other kids at school. My 'au naturel' horse chestnuts didn't put up much of a fight in the playground competitions.

While my dad ticked all the right boxes as far as me and my mates were concerned, Mum didn't hold him in the same regard.

When we lived in East Goscote, Dad worked at a mill on the very edge of Leicester for a company called Chapman Frazers. It wasn't a particularly skilled job – Dad was a foreman, responsible for putting the bobbins of yarn on to the looms to make the cloth – nor was it very glamorous. Dad took me to the factory once. It was scary and noisy. The looms seemed massive and the whole place was intimidating. Dad walked me proudly through the nightmare place and introduced me to a friend called Jim. I couldn't wait to get out.

When we moved to Melton, Dad changed jobs, much to Mum's annoyance. Her main problem was the reduction in pay which meant we got less money as a family. To this day she still says, 'Your father leaving Chapman Frazers was the biggest mistake he ever made.'

Dad's new employer was a publisher called K&R Books. Originally they were based at Syston, near where we had our day trips, but then they relocated to Edlington Hall in the Louth area. Dad's job was to sell the company's books about pets. Normally he had to travel to individual shops to do this, but every so often he would go away 'on business' for a few days.

On one occasion, when he'd worked there a while and had his feet firmly under the table, he asked me to go with him.

Normally I wouldn't have had any interest in Dad's trips, but this one was the budgerigar equivalent of 'Crufts' held at Earls Court exhibition centre – and my boyhood hero Geoff Capes was due to be there as the event's special guest.

At that time Capes was one of the biggest stars around – quite literally. He was the reigning World's Strongest Man and a giant of a human being. He looked like a bigger version of Bluto from the *Popeye* cartoons. He was quite a family favourite because he was an ex-policeman, which meant that my mum liked him as well.

What a lot of people might be surprised to learn, however, was that he was also a champion budgerigar breeder.

Dad's company had published several books on budgies and he'd met Capes several times, as well as plenty of other celebrities. Arranging a meeting with my hero would be easy, he said.

I couldn't contain my excitement at the prospect of meeting this legendary TV star, but as usual Mum tried to pour cold water on my enthusiasm. She wasn't at all happy about me going away with Dad. 'I don't want Duncan missing school,' she said. If I was ever sick she would still send me in, even if I was later sent back home for being too ill to be among other children. The next day Dad telephoned my headmistress, Mrs Cook, and convinced her that it was in my interests to skip Friday's lessons. 'I suppose it's all right,' she told him. 'It sounds as though it's educational.'

Not only was it educational, it was vocational. When I was a kid I wanted to be a vet, so a pet show seemed the perfect training place. Both Mum and Dad supported and encouraged my dreams, at least on the surface. We always had pets to play with and look after, and Mum was a huge fan of the James Herriot books and television programmes. I remember watching *All Creatures Great and Small* on TV and thinking, 'I want that life.'

My parents used to boast, 'He is going to be a vet when he grows up', to anyone who would listen, and I enthusiastically told people the same thing, given half the chance.

On the morning of the pet show, Dad and I drove down to London and divided the day between manning his company's booth, from where he was selling books on pet birds, and wandering around the vast hall. I had never seen so many people under one roof. There was so much to look at I wasn't bored for a minute, even though I didn't have any real interest in budgies and Dad was too busy working to pay me much attention.

I couldn't wait for the second day. According to all the posters, that was when Geoff Capes was scheduled to appear.

Dad had booked a room for us in a nearby motel. I had been in a hotel before, but never a motel. This one had tea- and coffee-making facilities in the room, and a television, and there was even an en-suite bathroom. I was bowled over by the luxury of it all.

I only had minutes to take in the grandness of my surroundings before Dad suggested we 'have some fun'.

I should have known the day's enjoyment could not last. My stomach churned like a washing machine. I knew exactly what was about to come.

But I was wrong. This time was worse. Much worse.

'Get undressed,' he said, and I noticed he was already removing his clothes. He made me face the bed, at right angles to the mirror on top of the large, wooden dressing table. I looked to my side and could see my own body in profile. Behind me I could see my dad, naked and physically aroused. I turned quickly away. If I could not see it, perhaps it was not really happening.

'Lean forward.' I felt my father's rough hands on my shoulders and he pushed me over the bed. I still kept looking straight ahead, down at the floor.

I felt movement between my buttocks and then a push as my whole body shuddered forwards. And then, for a few seconds, nothing.

I looked up at the mirror. I could see my dad's erect penis going in between my buttocks. And that's when I felt the pain.

I had never been in so much agony in my life. The sensations were sudden and confusing. I could feel a mixture of burning, ripping, stretching all at the same time. His penis was in my anus.

'Stop it!' I cried.

I looked in the mirror and I could see he was not moving any more. Dad was standing still with his penis still inside me.

Suddenly I felt him freeze rigid. Someone was rattling the door from the corridor. His hands pinched harder into my shoulders. I will never forget the look on his face at that moment. Absolute panic. When he realised the door was safely bolted and the visitor could not get in, he relaxed.

'Please stop,' I begged.

Once again he stayed where he was and did not pull out. 'Have you any idea how much money I could make from these photographs?' he asked.

What?

Then he grabbed my head and swivelled it towards the

mirror. Standing in the corner of the room, by the bathroom door, was a camera fixed on top of a tripod. A remote control wire ran from the camera to a plunger switch which lay on the bed in front of him.

Only then did he ease the pressure on my shoulders and pull his penis out of me. It felt like my insides were being sucked out. It was nasty and dirty. The pain did not stop.

I was pulled upright and guided through to the bathroom.

'Straddle the loo,' my father instructed, and I was made to put my legs on either side of the toilet bowl. Again he leant me forwards, until I was resting on the low-level cistern screwed to the wall.

He stood behind me for a few moments and studied the view. With my legs so far apart, he could see my small scrotum hanging down. Bending, he edged forwards and somehow managed to push his still erect penis between my legs until it nestled against my testicles. I tensed. 'I'm not using a condom,' he said. 'But don't worry, I'm going to come down the bowl.'

Looking down, I could see the head of his penis poking out underneath mine as he pushed, then disappearing as he withdrew. He felt hard and hot against me and I was aware of the sensation of his hair tickling me between the legs and on my back.

I felt sick. I started to cry. But at least it did not hurt, and for a few seconds I was distracted from the pain in my bottom.

I cannot recall how long this went on for. Too long, definitely, but it probably wasn't as drawn-out as normal. At home Dad's 'fun' usually lasted about ten minutes. It felt like forever, especially if I had to keep changing arms.

Eventually my father started to pant and make odd noises close to my ear. I prepared myself for the worst but I did not expect what happened. With short exclamations of pleasure, he pulled away from my scrotum and held on to my shoulders to steady himself as his penis ejaculated over the back of my left leg.

I couldn't see it but I felt it. I felt it down my thigh, I felt it in the crook of my knee and I felt it on my calf. Where were the tissues he always used at home? For some reason this freaked me more than anything else he had done. I screamed. I was in utter panic, hyperventilating wildly, not really knowing why.

I pushed away from the cistern, ran out of the room and jumped on to the double bed where the maid had lain two towels. I could not wipe his mess off me quickly enough. I was scrubbing viciously at my own skin, scratching it with the less than soft material.

From the bathroom I heard the shower start to run. Dad was washing. I pushed myself back on the bed until I was leaning against the wall. When Dad came out, he made us both a cup of tea and we spent the rest of the evening watching television in bed.

I couldn't wait for the day to end, but I was terrified of falling asleep in case the nightmares just made it worse. My bottom was so sore, it made it painful to lie on my back.

Gradually the pain gave way to tiredness. Just before I fell asleep my father promised, 'Don't worry, tomorrow night we will make it special for you.'

The next day I tried my best to focus on finally meeting my hero, Geoff Capes. I couldn't forget what had happened the night before, and I certainly couldn't undo the pain I still felt, and the terror it had caused me, but if I was lucky I could distract myself. 'I'm actually going to see The World's Strongest Man in the flesh, and not on TV as usual,' I told myself. 'I can't wait to tell my friends back at school.'

Putting the last twenty-four hours behind me was hard. Until Geoff Capes arrived, I had to sit with Dad in his booth while he sold books. Every time I looked at him I suffered flashbacks of the motel room. I forced myself to ignore the images and concentrate on what was to come. After all, Dad seemed to be doing a lot of business. 'Perhaps he will get a bonus,' I wondered. 'That would make Mum happy.'

Out of nowhere, my day was suddenly torn apart. One minute I was fine, the next I felt a terrible lurching in my stomach. It was so violent that by the time I realised what it meant, it was too late. My vomit went everywhere, over books, on the floor, down the front of my clothes. I sobbed as I was being sick and Dad didn't know what to do. Mum was always very good when we were ill. I suppose training as a nurse prepares you for all sorts of mess. Whereas Dad seemed more concerned about the state of his booth. Who was going to want to buy anything now?

I spent the rest of the day walking between the toilet and the sales stand. I was sick several more times, much to Dad's annoyance. 'Look at the mess you've made,' he said. 'Most of this lot will have to be chucked away. The day's ruined.'

He was right. I never did get to see Geoff Capes.

When we got back to the motel, I could not face any food. All I wanted to do was sleep.

Dad had other ideas.

'Come on, Duncan, give us a flick.'

'Is he serious?' But at least I knew where I stood with this act. I had experienced it so many times, more than I could count.

As usual we both undressed, but instead of going into the bathroom, as we always did at home, we climbed on to the bed. I was almost on autopilot as I lay back with my head on the pillow. My father knelt beside me and took my penis in his mouth. I did not enjoy it but I still felt my penis grow erect as he sucked. Sometimes I just could not prevent it, even if I thought of the most horrible things I could imagine.

I don't know why my dad enjoyed it so much. I thought it must be like sucking a ping-pong ball through a straw.

When I told him I was sore, he stopped. As usual. Then it was his turn to lie back while I got on to my knees and masturbated him. As usual.

My arm started to ache earlier that time because I was still so fragile from throwing up. All I could think about was wishing he would finish so we could watch television and go to bed.

Even though we were not in the bathroom, when my father snatched his penis out of my hands and threw himself over on to his left side to ejaculate, he had managed to line up sheets of toilet paper to catch as much of the mess as possible. Not all of it, though. Some missed the paper and landed next to it. Next to me. As usual.

5

I Never Wanted a Son

When I was eight we moved to St Michael's Close in Bill-inghay, Lincolnshire. It was closer to Dad's job at K&R, so the whole family relocated.

K&R was run by Dad's acquaintance Dennis. The pet books business was very lucrative and each new edition sold like hot cakes, making Dennis a very rich man. He bought a huge mansion house near Horncastle called Edlington Hall, where the company was based. Legend had it the place was haunted. Mum says she saw ghosts whenever she was there and always felt weird things going on around her.

Dad was jealous of his employer's success. While Dennis lived like a lord, our new house was slightly more conservative, even if it was a step up from what we'd had before. We lived in a square, detached modern house with a garden no larger than the East Goscote one at the front and about double that size at the back. A grand old willow tree stood on one side of the front lawn, and on the other side was a porch entrance. Above the porch was a small room, which was mine. Next to that was Mum and Dad's room, then behind that Johanna's and next to that the bathroom. As I said, the house was very 'square'.

Our Melton address was always very tidy, but Billinghay was the opposite. Mum was working longer hours than before and each room was filled with clutter, piles of old magazines and as much junk as we could possible live with. The attic was stuffed to bursting point as well.

When we moved in, my parents bought a brown three-piece suite for the lounge. It was second hand. Most of our furniture had a life before it came to us. Our sideboard and china cabinet were gifts from some distant relative but were welcomed by my mother as highly prized treasures, despite the cheap wooden panelling and broken edges. When an aunt died we received a truckload of her belongings which Mum somehow managed to squeeze in. My sister was given the deceased's bedroom suite, which she still has in her room to this day. We also acquired two grandfather clocks from another dead relative. Neither could tell the right time. 'They're antiques,' Mum said. 'They don't need to work.'

Virtually everything in my room came courtesy of dead relatives I hadn't met. My cupboards, the trunk, the units – you name it, I was given it. The only new thing of my own I ever had was my bed. When I was eleven, Mum said she couldn't sleep with Dad any more because he tossed around too much in his sleep, so she ordered two new single beds for them – and, while she was at it, one for me. Dad was out when they were delivered, so Mum and I struggled to lift them up the stairs on our own, two into their room and one into mine. The bed I had before that had metal springs on a metal frame and squeaked if you as much as coughed. The new bed was very comfy.

My sister's room was very spacious, with built-in wardrobes and drawers. Mum said that since I had the biggest room in Melton, Johanna should get this one. As much as I liked it, I was never given a choice about being put in the loft in Melton.

As a teenage girl, Johanna's room was a shrine to three men, Cliff Richard, Shakin' Stevens and Elvis. There was only one 'real' person in her life and that was Mum. Their closeness was nice to see, but it made me feel excluded. If it was just us three in the house, I felt like an outsider.

In the evenings Mum and Johanna would normally sit on the sofa while Dad and I had the two matching chairs. In Melton I would sometimes sit on his lap to watch television, but that stopped when we moved. Jo often ended up with her head in Mum's lap, sucking her thumb, while Mum stroked her back or hair.

Mum made a fuss of me when I was ill. Apart from that, she said, 'Cuddles are for girls.' Dad was not the tactile type either. When I did get hugs, it was in response to some achievement I had managed, or some act of kindness that was worthy of praise.

I guess my parents had their reasons for the different ways they raised us. I remember asking Mum once why Jo was treated better than me. In reply she said, 'You're strong, Duncan, you don't need me like your sister does.' Jo was a sickly child. She had asthma and was deaf in one ear, so she warranted more TLC than I did.

The bond between mother and daughter was very strong. They shared a lot of the same traits. Neither had any real social life. The only visitors who came to the house to see Mum had business reasons.

'The Man from the Pru', as he was called, put in an appearance once a week to collect money for various insurance policies. Both my Mum and Johanna had these little orange books that logged how much cash they had handed over. The idea was that they had to pay a set amount each month for an agreed period. At the end of that time they would receive a lump sum. Mum had an orange book for me which was supposed to be given to me when I was sixteen. I was eighteen when she eventually handed it over because she said at sixteen I could not be trusted with money. She may have been right.

Mum liked the visits from the Pru man. He always called in for a cuppa and a good old chat, and usually stayed for at least half an hour. It was the only time I ever heard Mum laugh with another adult.

My mother's only other regular visitor was the 'Avon Lady'. Again, she always made her guest welcome by inviting her into the house. As the years went by, however, and the saleswomen changed and got younger to her eyes, Mum started to keep them at the doorstep while she disappeared inside to look for her purse and that month's catalogue. The older she gets, the more convinced Mum is that she is going to be mugged in her own home.

My sister never had any visitors. She had one school friend, Lorraine Cross, but she lived in the next village so they didn't play much. Johanna never went out to play after school. I was at the other extreme, always staying out late whenever I got the chance. Mum said I was a 'handful' compared with my sister.

Once I was late in from school and Mum exploded with anger. That was nothing new. But this time she went further. 'I never wanted a son anyway,' she shouted.

I went upstairs and cried.

Years later I asked my mother about this exchange. She remembered saying the words but said she did not mean them that way.

'What way did you mean it then, Mum?' I asked.

She did not answer.

Apart from the posters, I don't remember Johanna's room very clearly as I was never allowed in it. By the time I was eight or nine, the age gap was really starting to show. The last person she wanted to spend time with was her little brother.

The walls in my room were covered in woodchip paper. I used to pick the flakes off when I was bored, which was quite often. There was a big bald patch next to my bed where the chips had ended up on the floor.

It's amazing what mischief you can make without leaving your bed. When I was nine I got into trouble for sticking my bogies on the underside of the lowest shelf. It was quite a collection, amassed over a few months. They were invisible to the eye of a standing adult, but one of Mum's cleaning purges eventually unearthed them and put a stop to my fun. I was ordered to clean the shelf and throw the bogies down the loo.

The downstairs may have looked like Steptoe's yard, but my bedroom had to be spic and span at all times. Mum's rules. It was not easy. I had a cupboard for clothes, three shelves on the wall and a steel trunk which was always full. The rest got pushed under the bed and scattered to all four corners of the room. It was impossible to do anything else in such a confined space.

Mum had a frustrating habit of vacuum cleaning my room as a punishment. She wouldn't warn me. Before she could clean the floor she would pick everything up and stack it in a tower on my bed. She would not say anything, so when I went to bed I'd find this mountain of possessions. Everything from under the bed, behind the cupboards, clothes, toys, the whole lot, all scooped up and dumped on the bed. The floor, however, would be immaculately Hoovered.

Other than clothes, I didn't have very many personal possessions. There were a few *Dandy* and *Beano* annuals on shelves, alongside a couple of big fossils I had found, plus one or two quartz crystals scavenged from one of our day trips. Pride of place, though, was a large submarine I'd assembled from an Airfix kit.

I really loved building those models. This one was my favourite. A Second World War veteran. I spent many happy hours constructing it on the oak dining table. Having made good progress on it, I went to bed, and the next morning discovered it was suddenly fully built. Dad had finished it.

I think he thought he was doing me a favour, but actually he took away a lot of my pleasure.

I tried to make my bedroom as much of a sanctuary as possible. I had posters on the wall of Status Quo and Nottingham Forest. I supported Forest for a while because they were local(ish) and they were top of the league. The main reason, though, was that everyone else did. Later I supported West Ham. Everyone at school had a football stickers album. We would buy packs of stickers in newsagents and swap duplicates in the playground. West Ham was my favourite sticker so I decided to follow them.

Both Johanna and I had 'treasure bags' full of goodies we accumulated over the years. My hoard was mainly book-marks, postcards and key-rings bought each year during our Trusthorpe fortnight or on one of our days out. Mum kept the bags hidden from us. 'They need to be looked after,' she told me. 'You've got some valuable things in there.'

When I was older I was trusted to display my key-rings on a piece of bamboo suspended from three hooks in one of the shelves.

My mother found my treasure bag recently. I think she was upset when I told her I didn't want it. 'But you collected all these things,' she said. 'It's your treasure.'

'It's just junk, Mum.'

We were given pocket money from quite an early age, but Mum monitored how it was spent. Each piece of booty in our treasure bags was approved by her. I remember getting five pence, then ten pence, then twenty pence per week. We also got ten pence from the 'tooth fairy' when our baby teeth fell out.

My piggy bank was in the shape of a book. You could hide it on a bookshelf, so a burglar wouldn't see it. It was lockable, but I found I could always get money out by waggling a pin in the coin slot.

I was encouraged to do jobs around the house for extra money, usually if something had to be done at short notice. Mum had a nasty habit of welching on our deals. 'I'll give it to you when we go on holiday,' she would say when I had finished her latest task. It always felt as if I had been tricked.

Johanna was never given any extra chores, but then she did a lot to help Mum anyway. She preferred that to playing outside or being with people her own age.

One of my jobs was helping Mum with the supermarket shopping on Friday evening. 'You're a big strong lad,' she would say, so I had to carry the boxes and bags to the boot of the car. That part was fine. What I didn't like was standing idly by while Mum talked to random people for what seemed like ages. If I wandered off I was scolded. I just had to stand there.

I also had to wash the dishes after dinner. Normally, as long as it was done at a reasonable hour it didn't matter when I did it, but sometimes Mum would decide that she wanted it done 'now'. I guess she had her reasons, but it seemed arbitrary to me. I remember one horrible episode.

'Duncan, do the dishes, please.'

'Mum, I'm watching *Top of the Pops*,' I said. 'I'll do it in ten minutes.'

'I want it done now.'

'But—'

'Now!'

The more I protested, the more Mum screamed at me. As I reversed through the kitchen door, Johanna gave me the most sarcastic of smiles as she sat down with Mum to watch the show.

Occasionally I would be given other tasks like cleaning the black mould from the grout on the bathroom tiles. Like a lot of things, I could never do it to Mum's satisfaction, so she didn't ask very often.

Being told off so randomly and so passionately made me feel closer to my father. He gave me a few odd jobs to do every now and then, but not often. Washing the car was my favourite. I had to use a sponge in a bucket to soap it down, but I was allowed to use the hose to wash the suds off, which was always messy fun. Sometimes Dad would get me to mow the grass. Not often, though, as he liked to do it himself. 'It gets me out of the house and away from your mother's nagging,' he would say.

I felt like an adult when Dad moaned to me about Mum. It was as if he was treating me as his mate.

My father was not really interested in the running of the house. There was only one chore he required of me. It was the same in Billinghay as in Melton. Identical, in fact – the things he did and even the things he said. I do not remember every time I gave Dad a flick, but then I do not remember every time I washed my hair. They were both just part of my tri-weekly bathing routine.

One evening soon after we arrived at St Michael's Close set the standard for many to follow.

On wash nights I would either be sent to the bathroom or, once I reached ten or eleven, I'd go up of my own accord. That's how it was this night. At some point during my ablutions Dad knocked on the door, just as he always did. I stopped brushing my teeth and unlocked the door. Just as I always did. He came in without saying a word, and in his hands was a copy of *Razzle*, the men's soft-porn magazine. Sometimes it was *Penthouse*, sometimes it was *Fiesta*, sometimes something else. Always the magazine was of the heterosexual 'top shelf' variety.

While I finished rinsing the toothpaste from my mouth, Dad sat on the toilet lid and started to thumb through the magazine. A couple of times he stopped to admire one of the women and showed me the pictures.

'What do you think of her, then?'

I thought she looked nice. I thought all the ladies in the pictures looked nice, although I never liked seeing their pubic hair. Not when I was young. I associated hair with Mum. Johanna and the other girls whose 'cracks' I had seen were bald 'down there'.

Then he reached the letters page. This was where readers wrote to the magazine about some incredible sexual exploit they had experienced. Dad said all the tales were made up. But he still enjoyed reading them.

He started to read one out while I washed my face. He recited it in exactly the same tones Mum used to tell me a bedtime story. Just as he always did. I listened, not able to follow what was going on in the plot. Just as I always did. And waited. Just as I always did.

Sometimes I would be in the shower when he came in, sometimes washing my face or hair or cleaning my teeth. It did not matter. He passed the time with the magazine, as if he was in a doctor's waiting room. On this occasion, as soon as I finished my cleaning routine, he dropped *Razzle* on the floor and stood up. Instinctively I lay down ready to submit to the usual masturbation and sometimes oral sex which followed. Then Dad said, 'Give me a flick,' and I knew my turn was over.

He unzipped the fly on his trousers and took out his penis and I did what I always did until I could bear it no longer and both arms ached from alternating between them. Dad was angry that I was tired. 'Come on, you can do better than that,' he hissed, and I felt disappointed that I had let him down again. But I knew he would carry on himself. He always did. I did not even squirm as he ejaculated on to the tissues on the floor. They were lined up in exactly the same place every time. I knew what was going to happen and where it was going to land. I had seen it hundreds of times before.

Sometimes Dad wore a condom. I remember the first time I saw one. The smell of the rubber was very potent on my hands after I had touched him. 'It saves me moving,' he explained.

When he wore a condom he did not need to line the carpet with tissues. He just stayed on his back with one arm covering his face as he climaxed.

I never enjoyed seeing his sperm. In a condom it looked worse, his white mess squishing around in the teat of this thing that smelled like a balloon. When Dad ejaculated on to the tissues there seemed to be gallons of it. I thought it would never stop coming out. I remember being surprised, looking at the full condom, to see how little there was in reality. On this occasion there was no condom. Eventually it was over.

It did not matter if Mum or Johanna was in the house or if we were alone. Exactly the same pattern. The same details, the same amount of toilet paper in the same place on the same patch of floor. And always the same language.

In a way that helped me get through it. The words, the actions and the outcome rarely deviated from the set pattern. It felt very familiar to me. It was not scary. I did not like it, but it was not scary. More than anything it was boring. The same monotonous ritual every time. I left the bathroom with arm ache. My father left with a smile.

Just as we always did.

6

You've Earned it

My father gave me my first orgasm.

I was twelve. We were in the bathroom at Billinghay and he was sucking my penis. I was not able to stop myself getting an erection, even by thinking of school and people I did not like. It was purely a physical reaction. It often happened to me, although my father did not seem to mind whether I got hard or not.

But this time was different. This time I felt a sensation I had never experienced before as my father's head bobbed up and down. I could not explain it. I was scared. Thinking I was going to wet myself, I panicked.

And then I climaxed. Into my father's mouth.

'Yes!' he shouted, and he punched the air.

That was the last time my father ever performed oral sex on me. I don't think he liked the taste of sperm.

That night I lay in bed thinking about what had happened to me. I had seen my own 'white stuff'. I did not take it in at the time, but my sperm seemed whiter than Dad's. His was yellow by comparison. Was that because I was young?

People talked at school about masturbating. Kids are obsessed with their changing bodies and discuss it among themselves all the time. I had never masturbated myself before, as some of the other boys had. I imagined that when the older boys spoke about it, they were skipping the parts where they father had tugged them off. As Dad said, 'Everyone does it, we just don't talk about it.' Our little secret was everyone's little secret.

From 1981 to 1986 I went to the Lafford Secondary School, a small, rural comprehensive which later had the dubious honour of coming in the bottom five schools in an Ofsted report.

Our uniform was black trousers, blue sweaters and white shirts. When you go to school, everyone looks the same. Regardless of what happens to you at home, you are equal in the eyes of the teachers and the other students.

I enjoyed school. Not the studying, of course. I was neither a winner nor a loser. I just was. I wasn't good at anything, but I wasn't bad at anything either. I was average – a C-grade student through and through.

But at school I was free. There were fewer rules than at home, and the ones they had were very simple. You had to be here at this time, somewhere else at another time, and behave in a certain manner. Teachers did not suddenly make up rules to suit themselves. Not like parents.

My mum and dad liked rules. They always made sure I did my homework. This consisted of Mum saying, 'Have you done your homework?' and me saying 'yes' or 'no.' They never checked what I had done and probably would not have understood it if they had. But an authority figure – in this case the school – had said I had to do it, and so they were keen to carry out the instruction. Rules had to be obeyed.

I was good at obeying orders. My parents had seen to that.

Unlike a lot of the other kids I never skipped school, not until my final year. Then we had double PE last thing on a Friday. No one really cared if you bunked off or not. I certainly didn't by then.

When I first joined the senior school I was perfectly conditioned for following directives. Some of my mates instinctively rebelled over every little thing. I was the opposite. I was trained to listen and behave. As a result, I have lots of fond memories about certain teachers. A few of them stay in my mind as the first adults who treated me differently from my parents. And that could only be a good thing.

Mrs Farmer taught biology. She was very strict, but loads of fun if you behaved yourself. Another entertaining one was Mr Wainwright. I used to pass on to him porn movies that my father had given me, and take others home. I recently looked on the website Friends Reunited and found this entry from an unknown boy in the year below me: 'This teacher used to let you watch porn films at break time.'

I feel guilty that they were the films I supplied him with from my dad.

My parents always attended open evenings to check on my progress. Usually it was Mum on her own, just like at sports day. Dad went occasionally, but he used the time to network other parents rather than to listen to teachers talking about me. He was not interested in seeing examples of my work either.

My parents' main reason for attending was to ensure they did not look bad. The phrase that I heard most from Mum's lips during the 1980s was 'What will the neighbours say?' For 'neighbours' you could exchange 'teachers' or 'other parents'. The idea of any Tom, Dick or Harry looking down on my folks was their worst nightmare.

So that's why I had to work hard. If I looked good, they looked good. They loved to sing from the rooftops about their kids' achievements. If I was a failure there was nothing to boast about.

Johanna was not a natural achiever although she always tackled her work very diligently. Where I got Cs, she got Bs. Hers were not the best grades in the world but they were good enough to punish me with. 'You're the black sheep of the family,' I was often told.

Shortly after I started at senior school I started to grow hair under my arms and around my 'private parts'. Puberty was an unknown quantity for me. Talk of sex was outlawed in our house, and that extended to all related subjects.

I remember once making the mistake of saying to a friend in front of Mum that my sister was sexy 'because she has breasts'. Mum went ballistic. She absolutely erupted. I didn't know what it meant. I was just using words I'd heard other people say.

Any mention of sex or anything sexual caused Mum to behave like a Victorian matron. Even when it came to our pets she resorted to euphemisms at every turn. I remember one occasion when I was with Dad taking our chihuahua Carlos for a walk. Dad was very gregarious. Unlike Mum, he enjoyed talking to people, and on this occasion he stopped to talk to an old lady in the street. I was bored, and clearly so was the dog. While they were chatting, Carlos started humping Dad's foot. As ever, Mum was embarrassed by the dog's behaviour. 'Carlos is randying again,' she said and tried to distract our attention.

It was not easy to ignore. That little dog would try to have sex with anything – cushions, the arm of the sofa, the cats, and on this occasion my father's leg. Without even looking down, Dad gave Carlos a kick to try to make him stop. It did not work and the dog continued. So Dad flicked his foot again and finally the dog climbed down.

That was not the end of it. Carlos sniffed around Dad's boot, circled it a couple of times – and as soon as I saw that I knew what was coming next. Sure enough, he cocked his leg and pissed on Dad's ankle.

I don't know if Dad felt it, but I made the mistake of giggling and I got a clip around the ear for my cheek. Poor old Dad was oblivious to his urine-soaked shoe. He thought I was laughing at something he said.

As we grew up, Johanna and I did not play much together, just the odd game of 'doctors and nurses' at Melton. When we moved to Billinghay we stopped holidaying in Trusthorpe. As a replacement Dad bought a touring caravan, and sometimes Jo and I played in it. When she showed me her crack again one day it was her own idea. 'I've grown hair,' she said. 'Do you want to see?'

It was weird. She looked just like Mum. Although sex was a taboo subject in our house, nudity was not an issue. In the summer we sometimes played without our clothes on under the sprinkler which Dad would put on the grass in the back garden. I would see my mother's nude body if she was showering when I needed to use the toilet. My father, of course, I saw naked virtually every day.

When Dad showed me porn in the bathroom I liked looking at the ladies' breasts. The hair was actually a turn-off. I remember several times asking Jo to show me her breasts, but she kept saying 'no'. 'I'll show you my fanny, but not my tits,' she said.

I was inured to nakedness because of the images Dad showed me in his magazines, although I knew I liked looking at the opposite sex from an early age. I did not realise it was a sexual instinct till later. If the opportunity presented itself to see a girl, however, I would take it.

Even though we did not have the closest of relationships – perhaps because of that – Johanna's burgeoning femininity intrigued me. I had a little mirror, about two inches long by half an inch wide, which I would use to look under the bathroom door when my sister was in the shower. This carried on for a year or two. Not every day, just now and again. I wanted to see 'real' breasts, not the paper kind Dad kept making me look at.

Mum's breasts were readily available for me to see any time she took a bath or shower. As sexual objects, they did not register to me, I don't know why. She was my mother. She was also old. She did not look like the pictures I saw. I do not know why I did or didn't like something at that time. I guess it was instinct. After all, something within me made me realise I was uncomfortable giving my father a flick. Something within me made me indifferent to the accessible nakedness of my mother. And something within me made me respond differently with girls closer to my own age.

I remember noticing one girl at school who was beginning to sport fledgeling breasts. For a while, her body was all us lads could talk about. If we were lucky, she would occasionally lift her top for our amusement. I think she was proud of the attention her changing body was getting her, although probably a little scared of the impact it created. In the summer we all congregated on the sports field and mobbed her until she flashed us what we wanted to see. We all cheered, then went off to play. I cringe when I think of how half a dozen drooling boys must have looked to her. At least, in our defence, we were all the same age. From our point of view, we were intrigued more than anything. The first kid in our school who wore a digital watch got the same mass inquisitive treatment for a while. He committed the crime of being different, just as the girl did. Nobody meant anything sinister. We had power through numbers; she had power through her own body.

I was afraid of getting hair because I didn't want to be like Dad. I don't know why I had this thought. It was instinctive. As much as I loved him, something in the back of my mind was ordering me to reject being like him.

I did not understand what 'coming' was. Dad talked about it all the time. It is what he called it when he shot his semen on to the tissues. 'You'll be coming all the time when you sprout a bit of hair,' he said. For that reason alone, I dreaded the day it started to appear.

I hated seeing his sperm. The arm ache, the magazines, the oral sex – nothing disturbed me like the sight of him ejaculating. It made me feel queasy. I never told Dad this. I just did what I was told, to make him happy.

Getting hair myself was a traumatic time for me. Dad did not like it either. Once the odd couple of strands started to appear around my groin he soon commented. 'You'll have to start shaving there soon,' he said. 'It's good practice for shaving your face later on.'

I thought he was joking. I was wrong. By the time I was beginning to look adult, he brought up the subject again. 'All the big boys shave, Duncan,' he told me. 'How do you think they get so much hair down there? Everyone knows it grows quicker if you shave it.'

And so I did. Or rather, I let him.

I didn't understand how shaving would make the hair grow back faster. To me it seemed a weird thing to do. I remember my father shaving my pubic hair one day when I was twelve. I barely had any worth mentioning, just a few tufts. But it made him happy. Not happy enough, though. I was getting older and things were escalating.

The shaving turned out to be only the first part of his plan. Once he was satisfied that I was baby smooth, Dad made me stand away from him while he attempted to insert his penis inside my anus. I wanted to please him, but it was too much pain to bear. I cried out, 'Please stop!' He was angry, but he let me go.

As I recovered my breath, my father tried again to touch me. He reached around my hips and pulled my penis and balls to one side. Then he placed his own cock between my legs and started to move backwards and forwards. I remember on this occasion he wore a condom. All the while he slammed himself against me he held my penis in his hand, away from the firing line.

I think he had planned to rape me that day, but for some reason he bottled out. Mum was in the house, so he was probably worried that my cries would have brought her running. Thankfully he never thought to use a lubricant to help him penetrate me. Looking back as an adult, I'm grateful for my father's naivety. If he had found a way to minimise my pain, I'm sure I would have been raped many more times.

Dad only shaved me on a couple of occasions. As much as he liked me to look smooth for him, I think he was worried that I might stand out at school. The last thing he wanted was a gym teacher saying, 'Why has the Fairhurst lad shaved his pubes?'

Puberty is your body's way of telling you it's time to grow up. Most kids are ahead of nature. There was no one at school who didn't try to act older than he or she was. It was all talk. The wrong word from a teacher or a too hard tackle during PE and the tears would flow as though we were four-year-olds.

One of the early 'adult' games we played at school was pretending to smoke. Pencils, pens and bits of twig were pretty good substitutes. Gradually one or two of the older kids started bringing in real cigarettes and matches. I was more fascinated by the ability to start a fire than draw on a fag, but for the sake of appearances sake I looked interested.

My mother has always smoked. It was nothing new to me to see people puffing away. Once my mates were experimenting, I wanted to try as well.

One day, when Mum and Dad were in the garden, I saw my chance. Mum's pack of ten was lying on the dining-room table. A lighter was next to it. Gingerly I took a cigarette from the packet and put it in my mouth. The dry taste was horrible. It also stuck to my lips, but I continued posturing.

'What do you think you're doing, young man?'

I hadn't heard my parents enter the room. I panicked at the thought of Mum going mad with me.

'He's having a fag, what does it look like?' my dad said.

'Well if he wants a smoke, he can have one.'

The next few minutes were very surreal. Mum walked over, took a match from the box and struck it. Then she held the flame up to the cigarette in my hand and said, 'Put it in your mouth and suck.'

I did as I was told. I didn't take my eyes off my mother. Any minute now I expected a smack.

But it didn't come. She lit the cigarette, I inhaled and, like so many first-timers before me, I choked and coughed.

'Keep going, son,' my father said. 'Stick with it. Hold your breath.'

I tried again and this time I vomited. I barely made it to the bathroom in time. Downstairs I could hear my parents laughing.

I think Mum knew I'd struggle. She thought that if I tried it so young, I'd hate it and that would put me off.

In that way she was right. But my father saw potential. By the time I was fourteen I was a habitual smoker. My main source was my dad. Every month he'd let me have a pack of ten, sometimes twenty. That was more than enough for me personally, but it gave me leverage at school. Not every kid has such a ready supply.

I didn't question Dad's generosity at the time. He was just being 'nice'.

The treats continued. Shortly after he made me 'come' for the first time, Dad announced, 'I've got something for you.' It was a small black-and-white television and, best of all, a shiny Betamax video player. Videos were the latest thing in the early 1980s. Only the richest kids in school had them. Gangs of lads used to pile round to their houses to watch 'pirate' versions of the latest film releases. And now I had my own machine.

The gifts did not stop there. Already inserted into the video player was my very own hardcore porn movie. For when I tired of that, there were a couple of others to watch later.

'You're a big lad now,' Dad told me. 'You've earned it. You enjoy yourself.' These were probably the same films I used to hand over to Mr Wainwright.

According to Dad, masturbating to porn was a rite of passage which I had gone through the day I first orgasmed with him.

The trips to 'tuck me into bed' became more frequent now. Even though my room was not as detached and private as at Melton, he stopped by more than ever. He liked to sit by the side of the bed while I watched the films he had brought.

When he touched me now, I knew that if I were not careful I would ejaculate again. This was not what I wanted. I filled my mind with all sorts or horrible non-sexual images to ward off the moment of climax. The more desperate I got, the more extreme the visions: dog mess, puke, blood, guts, violence, anything that was not sexually alluring. By doing this I could prevent myself from ejaculating. It did not work every time, but I always tried.

'What's the difference between sex and masturbating?' I asked Dad. I genuinely wanted to know the answer.

'Having sex with a vagina is the best thing in the world,' he said. (He did not say 'woman' or 'girlfriend', he said 'vagina'.) 'The orgasm is five times more powerful when you do it like that.'

I did not have a vagina. Why was he so interested in me?

Shortly after Dad made me climax for the first time, I started to experiment with my body on my own. Not in the bathroom, though. I waited until I was alone in my room. Sometimes it was while watching the television. Sometimes just using my own imagination. Soon I was able to make myself ejaculate. Dad was right. It felt like nothing on this

Earth. But I still did not like it. The semen that spurted out made me feel ill. It was like my father's. It reminded me of him. But it was a necessary evil. For the first time I realised that I enjoyed my penis being touched in that way. Perhaps Dad was right when he said, 'When you're older, you'll enjoy this.'

He asked me if I masturbated and I said, 'Yes.' There was no shame in touching yourself, he said. 'But don't let your mother catch you doing it. She'll cut it off if she sees you playing with it.'

According to Dad, Mum thought that playing with yourself would make you go blind.

Dad never suggested we masturbate together while watching porn. What I got up to on my own was my business. But while we were together, he called the shots. He dictated what I did to him and he decided what he would do to me. That's just the way it was. He was in control.

7

This One's Mine

When Dad's employer Dennis cashed in his chips, sold his books business and moved to America, the Fairhurst family fortunes changed for the worse. We still had bills to pay, and the only job my father could find was in a chicken processing plant. After publishing, it seemed like an odd move. Instead of dealing with clients and talking about decent sums of money for intellectually stimulating products, he was now working at a place where live chickens went in one end and burgers and fillets came out the other. Dad soon built up a reputation as a hard worker as a driver in the transport division.

Dad took me on his delivery rounds a few times so I saw the factory when he took his 7.5-ton fridge lorry in to be loaded. Dad always made sure I wasn't seen by his bosses. I think there would have been a few insurance issues if they had discovered a kid was travelling in his cab.

Forklift trucks were used to load the lorries, and the best driver of these little electric vehicles was a guy called John. I was always fascinated by the way he could whiz his forklift around inside these giant articulated lorries and never touch the sides. John was a jolly character and a bit of a comedian. He always had a kind word for me, which I really appreciated.

I thought Dad's lorry was huge, but in fact it was one of the smaller wagons. He and two other drivers, Stuart and Jock, would normally have to sit in the loading yard chatting over coffee while the giant artic' lorries were loaded first.

Dad's truck wasn't even large enough to be loaded like the others, so the forklift was no use. It was also too low to be reversed properly into the loading bay, so Dad and John had to stock it up manually. They made this into a game called 'handball' to relieve the boredom, chucking boxes of chicken to each other across the two-foot gap, along with a lot of banter. Sometimes I was allowed to help, but usually John would give me a cup of hot chocolate from the vending machine and I would have to wait in Dad's cab until they had finished.

Dad normally picked John up and dropped him off on the way to and from the factory. He got quite friendly with John's family, including his son who I'll call Robert. At nine, Robert was three years younger than me.

When the company downsized, Dad was offered the opportunity to move to a different department in the factory or buy his truck and go it alone. He took the latter option.

In hindsight it was probably a mistake. 'Your father could have been somebody,' is another of my mother's frequent phrases. He used to make similar comments himself, but only in private. Not in front of Mum.

Shortly after Dad went self-employed, John had a terrible accident. He was fixing the roof of his house when he slipped and fell to the ground. He survived but was signed off work.

Dad normally only ran one truck, which he drove himself, but at busy times he would hire another and John would step in to drive it. Within a year of his accident, John could drive and lift again, but only in short bursts.

For a while Dad continued to buy his chickens from his old employer, but when he found a cheaper supplier he quickly switched. I remember driving down to Smithfield Market in London with John during my summer holidays. We left at four in the morning and had to get in and out before the rush-hour started. While we were picking up, Dad used his small Bedford Midi van to make local deliveries.

I was paid five pounds for helping out on those days. That was a lot of money for me. I remember John's son being in the background when we were loading or picking up, but we never played together. At that age, the three-year difference was too much. Besides, he lived in a village five miles away and I was not allowed to cycle that far.

Dad now struck a new deal with the old company. They kept their large supermarket contracts and Dad would take over distribution to the small-fry butchers scattered all over the place. As a result he came across all sorts of characters on his delivery rounds. One of the most bizarre, and most constant, was a man I'll call Frank Dexter.

Usually Dad would pull up, drop off the poultry and move on to the next shop on his list. At Frank's, though, he always parked up and went inside for a cup of tea and a sausage roll or pie – always freshly baked on the premises.

For a kid helping out, stops like that were fun because they really broke up the day, and I really used to look forward to calling in on Frank. Apart from the delicious food he was the most entertaining customer I ever saw, on account of his inability to say anything without swearing.

'Good fucking morning to you, you fuck!' he would say

as Dad walked into his shop. Then he'd see me and say, 'How the fuck are you, junior?' and ruffle my hair with his hands.

He made me laugh but he also scared me a little. Once he grabbed my arm, held it to a chopping block and made as though he were going to cut it off with a cleaver. Because his apron was always covered in blood anyway, it would not have surprised me if he'd gone through with it. He didn't, of course, but it freaked me out. All the while he and Dad just laughed.

The only time I heard Frank speak without swearing was on one occasion when I was thirteen. Dad and I were leaving the shop after the usual delivery/brew/pastry combo and Frank asked my father, 'Cliff, can I have him?'

Dad stopped walking for a moment and wrapped his arms paternally around my neck from behind. He was about a head taller than me at the time.

'Oh no, Frank,' he answered. 'He's mine.'

Frank walked up closer to us and said, 'Go on, Cliff. It won't take long.'

Dad looked at his watch. 'Sorry, mate,' he replied. 'We're running late today. And like I said: this one's mine.'

And off we went to continue our rounds.

Despite the costs of Dad setting up his own business, we still managed to take a decent holiday each summer – as long as it wasn't during 'July fortnight', of course. With Trusthorpe increasingly a thing of the past, we started to venture further afield. In 1983 my parents decided we'd take the caravan to a holiday park in Dorset. By any standards it was a good week, but for us it seemed particularly successful. There were no major rows, the weather was good and everyone seemed to enjoy themselves.

For me the highlight was a visit to Bovington Tank Museum. Everywhere you looked there were giant pieces of military hardware. The main attraction was the collection of hundreds of tanks. I was allowed to climb on some of them and even get inside a few and sit in the driving seat.

From Bovington we drove to a nearby base of the Royal Signals regiment, where we were given a guided tour. I was completely blown away by the stories a sergeant told us. He made the soldier's life seem so glamorous and full of adventure – who would want to do anything else?

Certainly not me. On that day I ditched all pretensions to being the new James Herriot and working with animals. I was going to join the Royal Signals instead. That was my destiny. That was my ticket out of Billinghay and away from my family. 'I can't wait,' I thought as we left the base.

From then on it was only a matter of waiting until I was old enough.

The atmosphere in our house seemed to deteriorate on those occasions when we were forced together as a family for any length of time. Holidays normally combusted into a series of rows between my parents, which is why the Dorset trip stands out as being so peaceful. The other time when sparks would fly was Christmas.

You never knew when the fights would start, just that they were never very far away. There were arguments when the Woolworths Christmas tree went up and more when it came down. There were arguments every time one of the tree lights went out and more if anyone so much as looked at the presents before they were due to be opened. But the main fights came when the cats started playing with the baubles dangling from the fake silver branches – and eventually knocked the tree over. It was the same pattern every year. Mum would go mad, which in turn would set Dad off, and then that was it.

The fights weren't restricted to words. I've seen the turkey thrown across the kitchen, I've seen a cat kicked against the wall, I've seen Dad drink himself into a near coma. While all this went on I would drift upstairs and hide. Jo would normally curl up on the sofa, suck her thumb and try to pretend nothing was happening.

We all deal with problems in different ways.

The only things that brought us together each year were the Queen's speech and whatever James Bond film followed it.

While everyone seemed to have a torrid time at Christmas, I had another reason for fearing it. With time off work and the constant flow of alcohol, Dad's demands on my time in the bathroom always increased during the holiday season. He wasn't particularly more unpleasant because of the alcohol, but he was definitely more persistent. He also became more inventive in the ways he enticed me upstairs to the bathroom.

I remember one time when the four of us were managing to play Monopoly without too much fighting. As usual, the game seemed to be dragging on for ever, so Mum announced some new rules to speed it up and said that whenever anyone was out, they had to go to bed. I noticed immediately that Dad seemed to perk up at this news, and for the next ten minutes he seemed to be intent on making me 'bankrupt'.

It worked. I'm sure he was cheating but I couldn't work out how. Minutes after I'd left the table to get ready for bed I heard a commotion as Dad was conveniently declared 'out' as well. I counted to ten and, sure enough, soon heard his footsteps coming up the stairs.

Christmas was good to Dad in other ways. The weeks before the holidays were his busiest time of year at work. 'Poor people are good for business,' he told me. People who couldn't afford to buy turkey for Christmas dinner were forced to buy chickens instead. 'And since my prices are cheaper than the supermarkets' prices, they buy from my butchers!'

He liked lording it over the poorer folk. It made him feel superior, just as our holidays in Trusthorpe did. Both my parents spoke a lot about 'us' and 'them'.

Dad was a popular character in Billinghay, and his private poultry business just increased his appeal. He was always giving out frozen meat to locals to win their favour. It worked to a large extent, although like Mum he never had friends over to the house. Sometimes Jock, Stuart or Pete swung by on business, but that was it.

It was important to Dad that people thought he was successful. That's why he decided to go into business on his own. He was his own boss. Strangers automatically translated that into him being wealthy, and he did nothing to disabuse them of that idea. Dad normally dressed the part of the successful businessman, but in his whole life he only owned three suits: one black, one brown, one grey. Close inspection revealed that he wore cheap watches and scuffed shoes, and of course he only travelled in his van.

Apart from the way he dressed, another of Dad's tricks to appear superior was to always 'smell nice'. At least that was the plan. In reality he virtually bathed in Old Spice aftershave.

I could tell if he was in the house ages before I saw or heard him.

Even now the smell of Old Spice can still trigger some powerful memories. If I stroll near a 'tester' pot in a chemist's, or if someone walks past me wearing it, I freeze. Fortunately it's not so popular these days.

Among my friends my father was far and away the least 'dad-like' dad. As far as we were concerned that was a compliment. One of the ways he stood out among the other adults, although I didn't realise it at first, was his attitude to porn. He gave stuff to me and I showed it to other kids. Pictures of naked women are hard currency among inquisitive schoolboys. It was just like when I took cigarettes into the playground; suddenly I was important.

If anyone asked where I got my contraband from, I said, 'I stole it off my old man.' This was instinctive. Lying seemed easier than revealing the truth. The truth would mean admitting I was different from my mates. That would never do.

It never occurred to me at the time not to lie. It was instinct, like a defence mechanism. I understand now how damaging deceitfulness is to a relationship. But as a kid I had other priorities. My main concern was getting through each day, each afternoon, each hour. And if that meant twisting the truth to suit me, so be it. It didn't matter if I was talking to a stranger, a teacher or one of my closest friends. I said what I had to. Sometimes, I'm ashamed to recall, I said what I felt like. When you're so accustomed to avoiding the truth, it's hard to get out of the habit.

My father wasn't our only access point for dirty magazines. Bobby Davis was a short man with thick, milk-bottle glasses who worked at a local shop. Kids are harsh at the best of times and Bobby's looks gave us an obvious, easy target. He showed me and my mates porn magazines from behind the counter and often asked us to go round to his house. I have no idea what his intentions were, but Bobby's biggest crime was to *look* like a sexual deviant, whether he was or not. 'Kiddy fiddler', the older boys called him. I joined in as usual without questioning it. I never stopped to think what the term meant. I never stopped to think that some kiddy fiddlers might look like respectable businessmen.

Another guy in the village, Luke Allinson, also had a reputation for liking children a bit too much. We made this work for us. He might have been in his forties, he might have been twice our size, but if he was happy to buy us sixty fags and three bottles of Thunderbird cider on a Friday night (when we gave him the money), he was all right by us. He would be called 'learning challenged' these days, but to us he was this weird adult who liked to hang out with kids. I think he just liked the company.

I had quite a few friends while growing up, but the closest ones during my mid school years were Jim, Stephen and Andy. There were others that I called 'mates'. Tom, Rainy, Adrian, Steely, Scott and a few more all fitted into that category. When you're twelve, the difference between 'friend' and 'mate' is vast.

Me and my friends got up to all sorts of mischief in our early school years. As anyone who has lived in a village will testify, there is nothing for a kid to do. For a while we had a judo club, until the guy who ran it got locked up for armed robbery. We used to hang around the streets, entertaining ourselves in any way we could. All sorts of games, petty crime and mischief took place in the streets of Billinghay village.

There was a copper in the village called PC Graham. He was a nice guy, just doing his job, trying to keep the local kids in line and to teach us to respect the law. He had his work cut out.

A classic way of passing time was one of our recurring games called 'Truth, Dare, Double Dare, Command, Kiss or Promise'. It was an exercise riddled with confidence-testing potholes for those going through puberty.

In our gang the guys always outnumbered the girls by about three to one. There were an equal number of each sex in and around the village, so I guess the parents in Billinghay kept a tighter rein on their daughters. The game went something like this. One member of the group, usually the toughest, would challenge another member. 'What do you choose?' The second member would normally say, 'Double dare.' This was usually a wise move; get the worst out of the way early before everyone got worked up. The first would then choose the deed to be done. Examples included such orders as smash a window in the primary school, allow yourself to be punched in the stomach, drink piss and other random acts of insanity. Once the culmination was me and Tom setting off firework rockets down the road after a police car had gone past.

Another dare was allowing myself to get a fake beating near the main road. If it was done right, a passing car would stop and everyone else scarpered, leaving you in the road. Once or twice the good Samaritans offered me a lift home and I would sit in the passenger seat trying not to laugh. Normally they would just check to see if I was all right. PC Graham had his work cut out with us, all right.

Getting through the evenings and weekends was one thing, but just keeping your nose above water at school had its own problems. There was no support network in place at the Lafford back then. If you were lucky enough to have a teacher who liked you, you could turn to them. If you were just ordinary, like me, you were on your own. There were loads of bullies, as with any school. In fact there was an impressive hierarchy of thugs, constructed over generations. The older boys worked downwards, picking on the bullies below them. It was institutionally endemic. I bullied people younger than me in the same fashion I was bullied.

Being victimised for no other reason than your age or face or where you happened to be standing was a rite of passage among school kids in Billinghay. I had the usual scrapes, the odd fight and got into mischief with the teachers and other pupils. Nothing every kid didn't go through. I stood up for myself to the bigger boys occasionally but generally it was easier to take the thumping or the ridicule. If walking away earned me a term's worth of name-calling, so be it. It beat getting into trouble and having the school tell my parents. That's when the problems really kicked in.

Throwing your weight around was just something you did if you thought you could get away with it. I certainly did not think of it as bullying. Once a younger kid wanted to hang out with us, so we made him jump through a few hoops first. 'If you want to be in our gang you'll have to pick up a dog turd with your bare hands,' I told him.

So he did.

Once he'd done it we threw him in a ditch of dirty water and ran away laughing.

Our pranks were never sustained attacks on anyone or proper campaigns of intimidation. Usually it was just what occurred to us at any given time. Occasionally if someone went over the top with a victim smaller than them, me and my mates would intervene, especially in the final year when we'd often step in to rescue a first year from the clutches of a fourth year. But on the whole it was just accepted. We accepted it, they accepted it and the bully moved on eventually to someone else. Whoever you were, eventually the perpetrator got a slap from someone bigger which always brought them down a peg or two. We all got used to it. We were immune, almost. It was the way of things.

Like I said, boredom in a village finds a variety of outlets.

My father often provided a good distraction from the mundaneness of local life. Once he had started up in business as a sole trader he bought his own truck to drive around in. Sometimes he would take me with him on his trips in the school holidays, just like in the old days. If I was really lucky he would let me sit on his lap in the driver's seat and let me steer the van. We both knew he would get into trouble if a policeman saw us, which made me love him a little bit more. To think he would risk being told off by the law in order to give me a little bit of fun was incredibly inflating.

While I sat in the driver's seat concentrating on the road ahead, Dad would work the pedals with his feet and operate the gears with one hand. With his spare hand he would reach around and stroke between my legs. He was normally able to undo my trousers and slip his hand inside without much trouble. If I'm honest, I did not mind. It was not something that was alien to me and, as far as I was concerned, he was doing something special for me by letting me drive the truck. What he wanted to do to me was only fair. It was normal, after all. Normal for us.

The older I got, the more I began to notice how Dad was looking out for me. He often stood up for me in the face of Mum's wrath. When I was on the receiving end of a screaming fit about not having cleaned the kitchen floor, Dad strolled in and calmly said, 'It's my fault. I asked him to fetch my paper from the shop.' That stuck a pin in Mum's argument. Dad gave me a wink as he left the room. He had saved my bacon and given me one more reason to love him. He did this sort of thing all the time once I reached twelve. The older I got, the naughtier I got and the more he waded in to cover up for me.

'I asked him to help me load the lorry.' 'I said you wouldn't mind if he did it later.' 'I asked him to cut the grass.' These all saved my life at various times.

Our bond went beyond providing me with an alibi. Sometimes, for no reason, Dad would just give me money to spend how I liked. 'Don't tell your mother, there's a good boy.' It was often after a bath night, but I did not question it.

He also bought me a lot of good presents. When you're in your early teens, 'good' often means 'something that makes your schoolfriends jealous'. I had plenty of gifts that fitted into that category over the years, starting with my own video player. There were also bikes and other toys. Best of all, though, was my air gun.

'Fancy some target practice?' That was Dad's way of asking me if I wanted to go shooting. Of course I did. How many other kids were firing guns at my age? None of my mates were able to, unless they came out with me. I guess they were right. My dad was cool. Mum would have flipped if she'd known, but she never found out. 'We have to look out for each other,' Dad told me on one of our hunting expeditions. 'It's us against the rest of them.'

We would drive out to the country somewhere, find a big field and then aim at one of the trees. Sometimes he put tin cans or other bits of rubbish on a fence. The more noise the targets made when you hit them, the better. A lot of the time the only noise we made was the gun going off, but with practice the targets started falling. If I got a bullseye I would jump in the air and Dad would hug me.

Like any kid, I knew how to push my parents to the limit if I wanted to irritate them. I also knew which buttons to press to get what I wanted. Sometimes it did not work, but other times it did. And where my father was concerned, I knew exactly which buttons to push.

'Dad,' I said to him one day, 'can you buy me a catapult?'

I knew it was not worth asking Mum. In fact, I knew I had to be alone with my father when I made my request.

'I don't think your mother would like that, do you?' he replied.

'But all my friends have got one,' I whined. That was a lie.

'I'm not sure, son. They're dangerous.'

'I'll give you a flick.'

And that was that. He bought me a beautiful Black Widow catapult that smelled of leather and freshly carved wood. It was the latest technology in that type of weapon, and I had it. Thanks to my father. I knew if I offered to masturbate him I would get what I wanted. As he always said, 'You do something for me, I do something for you.' And it worked.

I remember the look on my father's face when he heard me ask. He was taken aback but happy. 'You're on, son,' he said. 'Race you upstairs.'

Our relationship changed that day. I discovered what I always knew really, which is how much Dad liked our bath times and what he was prepared to do for it. I felt guilty at the time. I had never heard of blackmail, but it felt like I was tricking my father into doing something. Mainly, though, I thought, as any twelve-year-old would: 'Why not? I'll be doing it tonight anyway. I may as well get something out of it.'

That was the first time I initiated physical contact with Dad. It did not bother me in the slightest. I was too used to it. I knew if I put aside half an hour for arm ache and boredom I would get the catapult of my dreams and my friends would be envious. As a kid, you have to get your priorities right.

8

I Was Four

I started stealing when I was thirteen. That was the age at which I got a paper round at the local newsagent. It coincided with my parents stopping my pocket money. 'You're earning for yourself now,' Mum said. 'Money doesn't grow on trees. You can start contributing.' The job paid well. But I found a way to make it pay even better.

The newsagent was based in a green hut near the church. Every weekend the owner would drive his van around the village to collect the money for the week's papers and all the paperboys would sit in the back, with their legs dangling out. That's why I wanted to be a paperboy in the first place. Whizzing about the village with your feet hanging out the back of the van looked such fun. It was a bonus that he gave me three pounds for my trouble.

At the end of the Saturday shift, the owner took all the leather satchels we carried the money in, cashed up and paid us our wages.

Either the guy never knew how much money he should be earning or he just didn't bother to count it. All the bags were cashed up at the same time, so how was he to know if my haul was a little light? One week I took an extra pound to see if he noticed. The next it was two, then three. Before long I was cycling home with an extra fiver in my pocket on top of my legitimate earnings.

It was the start of my slide into crime.

A few weeks later I discovered a couple of the other boys were nicking money too. Between us we were syphoning off thirty pounds a week. The newsagent never once said a word about being short.

Things changed a few months later when the paper guy retired. His business was taken over by the family who ran the sweet shop, and they had enough experience of cash-only transactions to block all the loopholes. Every penny was accounted for, and my 'earnings' diminished by almost two thirds. I needed to boost my income in some other way.

'But where is a kid going to get eight pounds a week?' I thought. And then I worked out the answer.

When I was alone upstairs in the house I loved rooting through the rest of the family's private belongings. I was like a magpie, attracted to anything shiny or interesting looking. Other people's possessions are just so much more desirable than your own. I used to play with Mum's jewellery and pretend it was pirate treasure. But only when she wasn't looking.

I was never actually told, 'Don't go poking through things that don't belong to you', but I understood instinctively to wait until no one was looking before I started my snooping. It gave me a thrilling sense of mischief. I knew it was naughty, even though I always put everything back where I'd found it.

Everything, that is, except money.

Mum always left her purse lying around the house. Sometimes in the kitchen, sometimes in the lounge. I was often alone with it.

It was the easiest thing in the world to unclasp its lock and take out the odd fifty-pence piece or pound note. Even easier to slip the money into my pocket and then carry on as though nothing had happened.

I knew it was wrong. I knew what stealing was, and I knew that that was what I was doing. But I also knew that Mum had money that she kept from us. If something caught my eye in a toyshop she would say, 'Put it back, Duncan, we can't afford it.' If I asked for new shoes, to be like the other boys at school, I'd get a similar reply: 'There's nothing wrong with the ones you've got. We can't afford to go around replacing things that aren't broken.' Always the same story: 'We can't afford this', 'We can't afford that.'

I saw her purse. We could afford plenty.

Sometimes when I raided Mum's handbag I had something specific in mind for the cash. But usually I took the money for fun. I stole because I could. Also, I think, I did it because I was sick of living under my mother's rules. I wanted to get back at her in some way that I couldn't otherwise express.

I started to nick from Dad as well. This was different. He handled large sums of cash in his business, and there was often a lot lying around. If you knew where to look.

'He's never going to miss a tenner,' I thought as I slipped my hand into the pocket of a pair of work trousers that I'd found slung over a chair in his bedroom. 'He's got thousands.' I doubt if he noticed. If he did, he kept quiet.

Later I got more ambitious. A tenner was not enough. Twenty wasn't enough. Whatever I could put my hands on, I took. He noticed then all right, but still he never said anything. He casually stopped bringing his takings home with him. Everything was left at the office or tucked away in a hidey-hole in the van parked outside.

Dad probably thought he was being clever. Unfortunately for him, he was a secret drinker. He would usually down a couple of slugs of vodka before he set off for home. He'd get in, scoff his dinner, then crash out on the sofa. It didn't take a criminal mastermind to rifle through his coat and find the keys to the van. My cashflow was up and running again.

There were occasions when I just wanted to stir up trouble. Mum hated how stingy Dad was with cash. 'Short arms, deep pockets' was one of her phrases for him. Anything for the home had to come out of the 'housekeeping' fund he gave her every week. There were no exceptions. I liked to take money from her purse and plant it in his wallet, hoping they would fight.

Sometimes I did it the other way round. If I went through Dad's closet eventually I'd find his wallet and it was easy to transfer a tenner into Mum's bag. I turned it into a game. To me I was the Robin Hood of Billinghay, stealing from the rich to give to the poor.

I don't know if they ever talked about what I was up to. They never spoke to me about it. I think I was trying to rock the boat between them, even if I did not comprehend why.

My relationship with my father had shifted. I can't put my finger on when. I sensed he was going out of his way to keep in my good books, but I didn't know why. Turning a blind eye to the stealing was great, but I knew it was weird. 'He must have his reasons,' I thought. Subconsciously I started to push the boundaries further and further. 'What's the most I can get away with?'

Around the same time a whole series of events started to

alter my outlook. The first took place one evening during bath time when I was twelve.

During one of our sessions in the bathroom my father asked me, 'Do you want to know how this started?'

When he said 'this' he made a sign of masturbating with his hand.

I don't know what made him bring the subject up. We hadn't done anything different. He had played with me and I had flicked him. Same old story. Nothing out of the ordinary at all.

'Yes,' I said. 'I don't remember.'

'You were little and we were having a bath together, like we used to,' he explained. 'I had an erection and you were fascinated by it. You said to me, "Why is yours big and mine is small?" So I told you about the difference between a limp dick and a hard one. That was the first day you gave me a flick.'

He said this proudly. I was confused. I thought I remembered the first time.

'How old was I when this happened, Dad?'

'You were four.'

I was four. Four years old.

My head started to spin. Why didn't I remember this? Why did I think I was six when it started? Why did I think the first time was that Saturday afternoon when Mum and Jo were out?

The more I thought about it, the more anxious I got. Even allowing for how young I was, I was disconcerted that I couldn't remember anything about that experience. Was it possible I had blanked it from my memory? That might explain why I had such a sense of impending doom on the afternoon that I do recall. I knew something was coming and I did not like it. It adds up. I believe my father's words. What would he have to gain from not telling me the truth?

'But why can't I remember that first time?' I thought. 'What else is my memory keeping from me?'

I don't think Dad expected his revelation to have that effect on me. To him it was a throwaway comment. Nothing would change between us. Why should it?

Worrying ideas were going through my mind at school as well. I had always thought that all my friends did the same things with their fathers as I did with mine. That's what Dad told me. I had no reason to doubt it. He told me no one would talk about it, and no one did. So if he was right about that, he must be right about the rest of it.

At junior school I didn't think too much about what went on back home. When I moved up to Lafford senior school it was different. Sex was on the conversational agenda virtually every day.

I never considered what I did with my father to be 'sex'. Sex was something that happened between grown-up men and women. I knew that much from our biology lessons. What we did was what happened between sons and fathers.

In my mind there was no distinction between 'gay' and 'straight'. There was just sex and that was not what I was doing. I thought all boys had done to them what was being done to me. It was loving. It wasn't sex, I was sure of that.

When I first hit puberty I had a crush on a girl called Tracey Black. She was just so cute, she fascinated me. Whenever I was near her I got a knot in my stomach that I couldn't shake off. I couldn't understand what was going on in my body. I would spend all day anxiously dreaming about seeing her and talking to her, and then go home and more often than not have to wank off my father. I didn't know I was having sexual thoughts about Tracey. I didn't know I was performing sexual acts on my dad. But I knew something wasn't right.

If anyone did something badly in the playground we called him 'gay' or 'poof'. The slowest runner, the kid with the worst hair, or out-of-fashion shoes: they were all offences punishable with the term 'gay'. I'm not sure we really knew what it meant. One of the other crimes that warranted it was if you played too much with girls. 'You prefer to be with girls instead of boys,' we'd cat-call. 'You must be gay.'

I don't think we really thought that one through.

Gradually, though, we became better informed. Every so often one or two lads would add to the group understanding of what it really took to be 'gay' and we started to build up a picture. For me it was a rude awakening.

'Gay men suck other men's cocks,' one kid said. 'They wank each other off.'

Everyone who heard it made the loudest 'urgh' noise possible. It was the law of the playground that anyone who didn't show repulsion at such descriptions must in turn be gay.

'Queers fuck each other in the arse,' another one revealed.

Another round of 'urgh'.

Outwardly I joined in with the chorus of disapproval, but inside my level of confusion reached new heights.

'I do that stuff with Dad all the time,' I thought. 'He does it to me. We've always done it. Does that mean I'm gay?'

I knew I wasn't gay. Gay men loved other men. I loved my dad, but everyone loves their dad. I didn't like any other men. I liked girls.

I liked Tracey Black.

I hid my home life well. I guessed my mates were all hiding their own secrets. If anyone else had mentioned doing things with their dad I would have been straight in there with 'me too'. But no one did. So I kept quiet like them.

I had another sign that I was not homosexual when I stayed over at my friend Andy's for the first time. Andy had the top storey of the house, which was divided into two. One part was where his bed was, the other was more or less a play area. It was full of junk, old books, toys and various hand-me-down rubbish from his older siblings. I don't think it was a special occasion. Andy's mum Janice had called my parents and said I was welcome to stay over to save them coming out to collect me that night. I was looking forward to it. It was an adventure staying away from home, even if it was in the same village.

Andy's bed was bigger than a standard single but not as wide as a double. That was where we would both be sleeping. Neither of us even questioned the fact that we would be sharing a bed. Talk of 'queers' and 'bum sex' was purely posturing for the playground. In private we were just kids having a sleepover.

I had no trouble getting off to sleep, but a strange sensation woke me up in the middle of the night. Something was touching the small of my back. It was skin.

I froze, I couldn't move. I could feel my heart beating silently in my chest. Minutes passed, and then Andy, who was sleeping soundly, moved again. I'm not sure whether it was a knee, a hand, an elbow or what. But it had the same result as the last time and I scrambled to get out of touching distance. All he had done was turn in his sleep, but I was totally freaked out and I couldn't relax for the rest of the night.

The next morning Janice said, 'Did you sleep all right, Duncan?'

'Yes, thank you,' I lied. How could I tell her I had flipped at being accidentally touched by her son? More important, why had I responded like that? Dad touched me all the time.

Was I now incapable of being touched by others? Would all human contact make me that jumpy? I was worried. 'Am I a freak?' I wondered.

I slept over at Andy's house on many occasions after that, but I always made sure there was an extra bed for me. If there weren't, I would make do with a sleeping bag on the floor. Anything rather than risk being touched inappropriately by a near naked boy again.

The more I thought about my reaction at Andy's place, the more I began to question my own home life. I was already making Dad jump through a few hoops as far as giving him a flick was concerned – the tacit acceptance of my thieving, the covering up for my laziness, the special treats. 'It's because he wants something from me,' I decided. If I was right, that gave me a bit of power over him. And so as a kid I naturally pushed that as much as possible.

Once or twice things didn't go Dad's way when he was after a flick. I remember kicking him in the balls once. 'Ouch, you little shit,' he screamed, and bent over with both hands clutching his testicles. That happened a couple of times over the years. Always accidentally on purpose. If he thought I was doing it intentionally I would have been smacked to within an inch of my life. I always remembered that time I made Damian the foster child cry, and being held up in the air by one arm while Dad thrashed my arse and legs with his spare hand. After chucking boxes of chickens around all day, lifting a scrawny kid was nothing to him. If he hit you, you knew all about it. There were times when it seemed as if I could get away with murder as far as my father was concerned, but if I got on the wrong side of his temper he would make sure I regretted it. Despite everything, he was in charge. He was the father and I was the son. As I knew only too well, he made the rules.

Andy's family lived quite close to the River Skirth. Just down the river, on the outskirts of the village, was a sewerage works. Next to that were a lot of stones, banked up, I think, as a precaution against flooding. Whatever they were there for, these giant pebbles were ideal ammunition for the Black Widow catapult I had persuaded Dad to buy me by giving him a flick.

For a few days I was the most popular kid in the village, thanks to this advanced weaponry. Everyone was envious and wanted to have a go. The main problem was making sure no adults found out about it.

Normally Andy and I would be happy skimming stones on the water and firing at random targets on the other bank. But one day things got out of hand.

We decided we would aim at a moving target. Even at our best we stood no chance of hitting something as small as a bird, so we picked the next best thing – cars.

On the other side of the river was a small field and a road. The chances of us reaching the traffic were practically nil because it was too far. But that did not stop us experimenting with various sizes of stone and a multitude of permutations of trajectory.

Ninety-nine per cent of the time we didn't even get close to the road, but the few times we did manage it were very exciting.

After idling away a few hours like this we were getting bored. 'Do you fancy heading off?' I asked Andy. 'Yeah,' he said, 'let's get out of here.'

Almost absent-mindedly I let one final stone fly from my catapult. With mouths open we watched as it sailed effortlessly over the field and on towards a passing bus. Even from where we were we heard the sound of breaking glass as the stone crashed through one of the bus's side windows.

'Shit, do you think you hit anybody?' Andy said.

'You were doing it too,' I said defensively. 'It was your idea.'

'You're the one who pulled the trigger. You're the one they're going to come after.'

Even as he said it I don't think Andy believed his own words, because he looked as terrified as I was. What if I had hit someone? I could have taken a woman's eye out for all I knew. What if anyone on that bus was dead because of us? Because of me?

'Imagine if we'd taken out the windscreen of a car doing sixty?' I thought. 'It was lucky we hit a side window.'

'I think we'd better get the fuck out of here,' Andy said, and so we scarpered along the bank and back to the sanctity of his house where, if anyone asked, we had been playing all day.

The next few days were terrible. We were paranoid about the police coming after us. The catapult was stashed in one of our myriad dens and we started working on our stories in case we were interviewed separately. At that age I thought that if you did something wrong, you got caught. It was later that I realised you really had to go out of your way to get the police's attention. For the moment, Andy and I were terrified of our own shadows in case they turned out to have a blue light on top.

A less potentially life-threatening game that took up a lot of our time was what we called 'hedge hopping'. In the early days it involved launching yourself into a nicely sculptured garden hedge just for fun. This gradually increased to seeing how many hedges we could bound over in one sprint. So from one garden to the next we would go hurdling over one beautiful work of topiary after another, trying our best to be as silent as possible. No one wanted to be discovered in someone's back yard. That was pretty much game over.

As a game it was short-lived in our repertoire of mischief, but it does explain why Billinghay could never have won Best Kept Village during 1983.

As much fun as reshaping an entire street's privet array was, we didn't really get much out of it apart from pure exhilaration. Another hobby soon replaced it, and this one was lucrative in a variety of ways.

The number one pastime for most of us young teenagers in the mid 1980s was shoplifting. We became very good at it, but then practice does make perfect. Between us, Andy, Stephen, Jim and I must have stolen thousands of pounds' worth of goods from various establishments of Billinghay. No shop escaped our raids, regardless of what wares they stocked. There was a time when we would steal anything that wasn't bolted down. We didn't even want the booty half the time, we were just doing it for the craic. We were bored kids looking for the next adrenalin rush.

One of our most daring hit and runs, although not necessarily the most profitable, was swiping a hanging basket from outside the White Hart Hotel in Lincoln, and this actually was bolted down (or up). The Hotel had its moment in the limelight recently when Tom Hanks stayed there during filming of *The Da Vinci Code*. When I was a kid, though, its fame was more as a holy grail for trouble-makers. You were doing well if you could make off with something from there.

Another pilfering highlight that sticks in my mind came a few years later. That was the night we stole a bench and table set from the local park and marched them through the centre of Lincoln to relocate them somewhere far more convenient. (They're still in one of my friends' houses to this day.)

School holidays were the worst times for us, but weekends and after school hours could also easily turn into opportunities for mayhem given the slightest provocation. Everyone was as bored as everyone else. I went along with the fun and games because it made me feel alive inside. It had never occurred to me before, but nothing in my life up until then had the same effect. Being with my friends meant the world to me at thirteen. At the other end of the emotional spectrum, going home each night became harder to face. Mum's rules, Dad's demands, the feeling of insignificance – it was getting more difficult to cope with.

Although I escaped punishment for the catapult episode, at other times I wasn't so lucky. My first juvenile run-in with the law, other than a ticking-off from PC Graham or another passing copper, was actually for 'receiving stolen goods'. Given the amount of sticky-fingered shopping in the village, it was only a matter of time. The contraband in question was a box of Cadbury's Roses chocolates which I had bought from a mate at school. I knew he had broken into a warehouse to get them, but that didn't stop me from giving them to Mum and Dad for Christmas. Unfortunately the chocolate factory raid was big news among adults, and they quickly worked out how I'd come into possession of the Roses.

My next caution was for something slightly more serious: 'possessing ammunition without a licence'. It wasn't as bad as it sounds, although the police didn't seem to think so. A few of us managed to get hold of some shotgun cartridges. We weren't intending to do anything nasty, as we didn't have a gun. But we were nothing if not innovative, and we soon had the cartridges cut open and the gunpowder poured into neat lines which we called 'genies'. To us it was just like something out of *The A-Team* or a *Road Runner* cartoon. We lit one end of the gunpowder trail and watched as the fizz of fire snaked its way across the grass. There was no massive explosion at the end, but that didn't make it any less exciting.

Unfortunately the police took umbrage at the number of empty cartridges strewn all over the village and decided to clamp down in case someone got hurt. For all they knew, there was a mad gunman on the loose in the neighbourhood. Somehow I was the one caught with the gunpowder on my hands and, despite the fact that there were at least half a dozen of us involved, it was me who was fingered as the Guy Fawkes of Billinghay and marched to the police station for the ticking-off.

We got up to all manner of naughtiness, but shoplifting remained the number one occupation for me and my mates. After a while, however, it stopped being a heart-racing end in itself and became the means to a very different high. We weren't just nicking stuff at random for the sake of it. There was one thing we all wanted in particular.

Glue.

Glue-sniffing among young kids was all the rage in the

1980s. I don't remember who did it first but soon we were all at it. Some of us did it to look clever. Some because they liked the buzz. And some because it helped drown out the grim realities of their daily life.

I quickly realised I was in the latter camp.

9

Never Again

While meals in the Fairhurst household were often fraught with tension as the four of us struggled to get on, many of our happiest times as a foursome occurred later in the evening, when we all slumped in front of the television. We were all in the same room, but the flickering box in the corner meant we didn't have to talk to each other. On the contrary, a word out of place during one of my parents' favourite programmes would earn a vicious 'Shh!'

These evenings of 'happy families' were not without controversy, however. When I was thirteen, I remember us watching a news programme together. The subject was child abuse and 'paedophiles'. I'd never heard the word before. I don't think any of us had. The newscaster read out a few horrible statistics about children being kidnapped, raped or abused in their own home. As a family we were horrified.

My father reacted first. 'They should lock them up and chuck away the key!' he shouted at the screen. 'Cut their balls off, that would teach the bastards.'

'Clifford – mind your language,' my mum stepped in.

'It makes me sick,' he continued. 'These perverts. Death's too good for them.'

Mum agreed with that, even if she didn't like Dad's choice of words. But I was perplexed.

'What's the old man shouting at the telly for?' I thought. 'These "paedos" that he's going on about are just doing what he does to me. What's the difference?'

I could tell from Dad's red, angry face that there must be a difference, but I was damned if I knew what it was.

But the seed was sown. 'Is he telling me the truth about what we do to each other when we're in the bathroom?' I wondered. 'Is the BBC lying to me? Or is my father?'

I couldn't even begin to understand the questions I was asking myself. Answering them was an impossibility. For now at least.

What if my fears were correct? What if I was being 'abused', as the TV people were calling it? That couldn't be right. But what if it was?

What if?

Thanks to the work of organisations like Childline in the UK and increased public understanding, children today have greater access to help. Things were different back then. As a young teenager in the 1980s I could see only one option: avoidance. 'If I keep my head in the sand, I'll be all right,' I told myself. 'If I ignore my fears, they'll go away.'

There was only one problem. The questions I didn't want to ask were never far from my mind. I wasn't strong enough to keep them at arm's length by myself. I needed help. Fortunately, I knew where to find it.

The high you get from sniffing solvents is extremely powerful. It also provides hallucinations every bit as vivid as those from LSD. Whereas LSD encourages users to imagine that inanimate objects have come to life, glue has a more pervasive and other-worldly effect. After the beginner's initial ringing in the ears has subsided, it proceeds to affect your vision, your co-ordination and your general everyday perceptions of things around you. But, more than that, it stimulates users into seeing things that couldn't possibly be there.

Some of the most beautiful sights I've encountered in my life have come as a result of sniffing glue. Exquisite sunsets, birds of unimaginable colours, visions of friends laughing so hard I thought they'd die – the experiences are as vivid as they are unreal.

Not all hallucinations are positive, however. The fear conjured by your own mind knows no bounds. But whatever monsters my deepest-rooted anxieties may have created, it never stopped me sniffing. I've sweated in panic at a glue-induced nightmare one minute, then filled another bag and inhaled again moments later, still wet with perspiration.

The alternative to facing the worst hallucinations didn't bear thinking about. That alternative meant facing up to my real life. It meant facing up to the fears I was having about my father's behaviour towards me.

'I know I must have got it wrong,' I reasoned with myself. 'He's my dad. He wouldn't do anything to hurt me. I should be ashamed of myself for thinking he would.'

If I said it enough times, I thought, I would have to believe it. But until then, there was always glue.

Getting hold of solvents to sniff was not that hard. Any local shop would sell you the stuff, and if they wouldn't then you could nick it. When the glue-sniffing problem reached the TV news, some stores did clamp down on the amounts a kid could buy. So then we just asked for puncture repair kits. No one would refuse a boy with a flat tyre, would they? Or an

Airfix model kit, Tipp-Ex or Tipp-Ex thinner, or Evostick or any number of other seemingly innocuous purchases. You'd be surprised at how many normal items come with their own built-in drugs supply.

Over time we went through the whole lot. Anyone who introduced a new substance to the group was 'the man' for a while. Sometimes, experimentation was as exciting as the high itself.

Gradually, one by one, each avenue was closed to us as vendors became more aware of the problem. But there was always Woodward's.

Woodward's Shop was the main supplier of contraband to the under-aged. We never nicked from Woodward's. We never needed to. The owner would, in reasonable amounts, let us buy booze, fags and let us rent blue movies. The glue he would ration, though, and the same with the lighter gas, which we moved on to next. If he saw the same face too many times in a week he would put his foot down, or if you came in with an order for ten cans even he would get a bit suspicious.

Glue-sniffing has always received a bad press, and rightly so. We didn't appreciate it at the time but it's very dangerous. The effects of heroin, cocaine, hash and acid are widely documented. So widely documented, in fact, that people who have never taken them can often give a passable account of their effects. But how many people actually know what glue does to you, and how you feel when you're on it?

A lot of us used glue at one point, but most people drifted away. They became aware of the risks or they moved on in their lives. I knew that substance abuse could kill me, I had seen the articles in the newspapers. But I had no choice. I had nothing to move on to. For three years, until the end of my school life, it was the only thing that kept me sane.

Jim was my main partner in crime. He was the guy who introduced me to glue in the first place, and we used a lot together and did many ridiculous and dangerous things as a result. But there were also good times.

One night we decided to sniff glue behind the wall in the old cemetery. That was a regular haunt when we weren't hanging out on the riverbank. We were fully prepared with plastic bags to inflate and supplies to pump into them. We'd been on a bit of a spree and got away with four new puncture repair kits and now we were really looking forward to getting fucked up. There's no real reason to be walking near the church with several bags under your arm that late at night, so when a girl we knew, called Annie, bumped into us she immediately deduced we were up to no good.

'What are you doing?' she asked.

'Nothing,' Jim said.

'Doesn't look like nothing. Where are you going? The church?'

I think we must have had guilt written all over our faces. Either that or she was telepathic. Her next questions blew us away.

'You sniffing? Can I come along?'

And that was that. The last thing Jim and I wanted was to share a single breath of our supplies with anyone, but our usual paranoia about being caught meant we had to buy the girl's silence.

Every secret has a price. I should have known that.

After a while of sniffing glue, it loses its potency. You have to top up or change bags. We had enough for a really good session, but after the first round of bags Jim decided to up the ante.

'Are you up for some more then?' he asked.

'Have you got any more?' Annie asked. I gestured to the other bags on the grass. 'Go on then,' she said. 'I'm in.'

'You'll have to do something for us though,' Jim said.

She looked suspicious. 'Like what?'

'Show us your tits and you can join in the second round.'

I had no idea Jim was going to say that, but the excitement was incredible. Eventually Annie agreed. She wanted to get high as much as we did. And the effects of the first bag had put her in an amenable mood to say the least.

We proceeded with the next round. I went first, Jim took the second go and then we passed the bag to Annie. It only takes a few seconds for the initial hit to wear off, and so we were on a down as she was going up. True to her word, she lifted up her top and Jim leaned over and pulled down her bra. Even in the state I was in, seeing a developed, young female form for the first time took my breath away. I was surprised at how fully grown she was and, even with no experience, I acted on instinct and moved in, latching my mouth around one nipple, my hand squeezing her breast. Jim did the same to the other one, and all the while she carried on sniffing glue.

At that moment I wanted the world to stop spinning and to stay in that position for ever, but eventually the glue lost its potency and Annie batted us off.

I had seen plenty of breasts in porno mags, courtesy of my father, but these were the first real ones I had ever experienced and somehow I was disappointed they didn't look like the ones in the pictures. That didn't stop me being highly aroused, and from that moment on I had a new teenage obsession.

Annie was my new love. She had let me suck on her breast and I couldn't wait to do it again. Unfortunately I would have to wait another year and a half for my next similar experience.

I didn't have to wait very long for the next glue-sniffing session, though. By now it was almost a daily occurrence. Every opportunity I got to fill a bag, I took. I didn't physically need company to get high, but if someone else was around I could convince myself I was doing it for fun. I could block out the real reasons for another day. 'I'm just having a laugh,' I'd tell myself.

At some point we made the switch from glue to petrol, and then to gas, which, strangely enough, was easier to get hold of – at least it was if your parents owned a caravan which was powered by butane.

Both my family and Stephen's had these vans, so we divided our time between the two. As far as our folks were concerned the three of us were harmlessly playing MERP, a Dungeons and Dragons-type role-playing adventure game based on Tolkien's *Lord of the Rings*. What they didn't know is that thanks to the 'on tap' supply of gas in the mobile home, we thought we were actually in Middle Earth with Frodo and friends.

Even our other mates didn't know what we were really up to. If word had got out that we had a private supply of butane in hundredweight bottles while others were scrapping around with lighter refill cans, there would have been a queue outside like at a seaside ice-cream van in summer.

One thing about sniffing gas is that it affects your vocal chords. Sometimes after sniffing a good bagful your voice drops lower and lower, until you sound like Darth Vader with a hangover. Whenever that happened it would crack us up and we would fall about laughing, just as we did if someone inhaled helium from a balloon. It was yet another reason for us to enjoy it, but it was also a potential give-away if someone who knew about these things heard you.

On one summer's afternoon we were at Stephen's and, when we hadn't been seen for hours, Stephen's mum came out to the caravan. It was lucky that she wasn't smoking when she flung open the door because the van stank of gas and we would all have gone up. Somehow she didn't seem to notice the smell, possibly because Stephen happened to be using the chemical toilet in the small bathroom at the time and that always whiffed a bit.

I forget what his mum wanted – something about dinner, I think – but it needed an immediate answer so she spoke to him through the door. 'If he didn't need a piss before, he will now,' I thought. When we heard his voice, Andy and I collapsed on to each other with laughter. It was like listening to Barry White, not some fourteen-year-old kid. I can only imagine Stephen's mum thought he was showing off in front of his mates, because she tutted and left us to it. I do know that if she had suspected the truth an exploding caravan would have been the least of our worries.

One of the things I liked about solvent abuse was how it blocked things out. When I was high, I didn't have to think or try to escape from anything. I was too numb. I didn't feel anything at all, good or bad. I was just content. Absolutely blissfully content and unaware of anything else in my brain for those few moments.

When I came down from a session the usual first thought I had was 'Fuck, I'm in trouble – I'm late home'. Sniffing glue or gas puts you in the kind of bubble where only those in the bubble with you exist. You forget about those outside. And you forget about everyday things like time. It's not a conscious decision. It just ceases to be in your thoughts.

Sniffing leaves its physical and behavioural traces, though, and soon we were coming up with excuses to explain our spotty mouths or unpredictable mood swings. We got into more trouble trying not to be discovered than by actually committing crimes. My parents filed everything I got up to under 'teenage rebellion' and thought no more about it. It was a similar story with the others. My fellow users would all compare stories about how they were nearly caught and the lies they told to cover up. In a way that made me feel better about my own life. They were becoming like me.

I don't know when I started lying to my mates. It wasn't really lying at first. At the start I was just covering up where I was getting my pornos from, or what I was really doing after school. If one friend asked me out in the evening I knew I couldn't reply, 'I can't, I'm wanking my dad tonight.' So I'd come up with something else. If I picked the wrong thing I'd get stick later on, so it had to be plausible.

'I can't, I'm going into town with Jim,' I'd tell Stephen. Jim never knew anything about it. Stephen never suspected. Not at first, anyway.

I had to be more careful with Andy. Because we used his house as a base so much, he was naturally the leader of our pack and he hated to be left out of anything. If Andy discovered we'd dared to have fun without him he could sulk for days.

Where he was concerned, I had to be very confident my lies were watertight. Sometimes, I'm afraid, they weren't.

'You're such a fucking liar,' he told me once.

It was over nothing really, just where I had been the night before, but he was right. Looking back, I guess he'd picked up on a few too many inconsistencies in my stories, although that was the first I knew about it. It takes a lot to stop kids playing with each other, though, and this confrontation didn't break up our friendship, but it did give me a jolt. I was genuinely shocked that he'd noticed I was lying. It was such second nature to me by now that I wasn't even aware of it myself.

I don't know if Andy mentioned it to the others, but I realised I was beginning to get a bit of a reputation. I often didn't show up when I'd promised. The amount of money I could produce at any one time fluctuated as well, depending on how drunk Dad was when he hid his takings. I never liked to say I was thieving from my old man, so on a barren day I would say I'd spent it on something else.

Small lies, all the time, and really only to cover my own tracks. But over the months these small lies combined to form a picture of a shifty customer who couldn't be trusted. I prayed that my mates would never realise this, despite the clues.

Could I blame them if they did? Like so many things, I didn't want to think about it.

I was no closer to learning the answers to my questions now than I had been when Dad declared a death sentence for all 'perverts' months earlier. What I did know was that there had been no let-up in our bathroom encounters since. If anything, Dad had got even more persistent in his requests. But that's life, I tried to reassure myself. That's normal family life.

'What paedos do must be different, or we wouldn't still be doing it,' I repeated again and again.

More than anything, I wanted to believe that.

When I was fourteen our school was involved in a foreign exchange with a class of students from France. Billinghay had never seen anything like it. Our secondary school served villages as far afield as Martin, Timberland and Walcott – we'd never had anyone from Paris before.

I don't know how the girls felt about it, but us boys were in shock from the moment the left-hand-drive coach pulled into the playground car park. Pressed up against the window in our form room we all agreed: 'French girls are beautiful!'

They really were cute, and when you heard them speak they just got doubly desirable. All the visitors needed local homes for the duration of their stay, so I pestered Dad to let one live with us for the week. I chose my moment carefully. During one of our bathroom sessions, just when I had him where I wanted him, I posed the question. I think he would have agreed to anything at that second and he quickly said yes. Then he had to persuade Mum. Eventually she caved in too and the arrangements were made. I was about to get my own Parisian beauty to play with.

At least that's what I thought. Dad probably thought so too. Sadly the person who actually turned up was the biggest dork in the world. Worst of all, it was a boy. Not only was he ugly, he didn't have a cool bone in his body. Even the other French kids used to make 'cow milking' hand gestures behind his back which was the universal signal for 'wanker'. The only good news was that in return for our hospitality I would be eligible for all the trips our French guests went on. Even better, though, was the fact that us host kids would get to go to Paris in exchange.

At the time, my father's demands were becoming increasingly frequent and more rough. 'Put some fucking effort into it,' he snapped once when I was flagging. 'For Christ's sake, Duncan, a girl could do better than you.' The idea of a week out of the country and away from him was more attractive than ever. One night in particular decided me.

It was the usual story. Dinner had been consumed in silence and I had washed the dishes. As I stood at the sink I tried to remember the feeling of being high on butane. If I could picture it in my head, perhaps I could escape from the tedium at home.

Dad had come in from work in a bad mood. The smell of vodka was apparent on his breath, even after he'd washed for dinner. His 'secret' drinking habit wouldn't have fooled Inspector Clouseau. Mum seemed oblivious to it, though.

After about an hour in front of the television I took myself upstairs. I was just getting ready to step into the bath when the door opened and Dad walked in. 'Oh no,' I thought. 'Not again. It's been every night this week.'

'All right, lad,' he said, 'give me a flick will you?'

Without even looking at him I shook my head and said, 'No. I don't want to.'

I think the answer took a while to sink in. There was silence for a few seconds and then the sound of the first stages of hell breaking loose. But I didn't care. Not this time.

'What are you playing at?' my father snapped. 'Are you going to be nice to me or not?

'No,' I repeated. 'I don't want to.'

That was the wrong answer. He flipped and, without

saying another word, pushed me hard up against the bath-room wall.

'Ow!' I screamed. 'You're hurting me.'

It didn't matter. With my face pressed against the wall and my hands leaning on the radiator below, I was aware of him scrabbling around behind me. Then he let go of my head and I felt one hand on my hip as he pulled me violently backwards. At the same time I felt the end of his penis push painfully into my anus.

'Stop it!' I shouted. 'Let me go!'

My words had no effect. I nearly vomited in agony as he pushed again and I felt more of his penis enter me. The burning sensation will stay with me for ever. So will the feeling of being ripped apart. Most of all, though, I'll never forget the sound of his panting and the feeling of his breath against the back of my neck. It was like listening to a forest animal attacking food. At that moment I felt like dead meat. I wished I was dead.

In and out he went, and each new time hurt more than the last. I began to hope he'd pull out and just rub his cock between my legs the way he often used to. Anything would be better than this. But that never happened. In and out. In and out. Wordlessly and painfully, with just the noise of his grunting in my ear as accompaniment.

After about two minutes he finally pushed his palm on the small of my back and withdrew from my arse. The next thing I felt was the hot liquid of his sperm as he ejaculated over the top of my thighs and backside. Again, it was all I could do to keep from vomiting there and then.

I looked behind me and saw my father wipe the end of his penis with tissue. His pants and trousers were around his ankles. He pulled his clothes up and left the room, still without saying a word.

When he had gone I rushed to lock the door and then threw myself at the toilet. I couldn't decide which end was going to explode first. 'Am I going to vomit or shit?' I thought, but as the burning was worse in my backside I sat down.

It was the weirdest feeling. I felt like I desperately needed to go to the toilet, but nothing came out. There were a few squirts and noises but that was it. When I went to wipe myself I got the shock of my life: the tissue was bright red. My arse was bleeding.

Panicking, I wound sheet after sheet of Andrex around my wrist and then stuffed the lot up my bottom until they stayed there on their own. 'What's happening to me?' I wondered. 'Am I going to bleed to death?'

I sat there for a long time, sobbing, terrified that I was dying and more confused than ever. 'Is this really how he shows he loves me? Do you nearly kill the people you love the most?' I asked myself. But, angry and upset as I was, in the back of my mind I knew it was my own fault. 'I shouldn't have said no. It was wrong of me. He only wanted to show me he loved me.' So many thoughts were whirling through my mind at once. What was the truth? Was it really my fault? Was it his? Will I be all right?

After about half an hour there was a knock on the door. It was my father.

'Are you all right, Duncan?' he asked.

'Yes,' I lied.

'Good lad,' he said, and I heard him walk away.

'See, he does love me,' I thought. But I wasn't convinced. Not any more.

*   *   *

Something changed that day. I didn't realise it immediately. The only thing on my mind as I heard my father walk back down the corridor was fear about the bleeding. 'I can't go to school like this,' I worried. 'How am I going to tell Mum what is wrong with me?' There were two doctors in our village, but one in particular was really nice. 'I can't even face telling him, though,' I thought.

I knew I couldn't tell anyone. 'I've already made Dad angry once today,' I was ashamed to admit. 'I don't want to cause any more trouble.' But if the bleeding didn't stop, I'd have to let someone know.

Just before I went to bed, I tried again to go to the toilet. The burning sensation remained, and my stomach still seemed to be churning over as if I was suffering from a bad case of nerves. But the bleeding had stopped.

As I lay in bed that night I started to think back to the events of earlier. I knew I shouldn't have said 'no' to my father. I knew I shouldn't have upset him like that by being rude.

'But that doesn't give him the right to hurt me, does it?' I reasoned. Mum smacked me when I was naughty, and Dad sometimes dished out the odd whack, but that pain vanished almost as soon as it arrived. The shock of either of them lashing out, and the suddenness of it, was almost as painful as the slap itself.

This was different. The pain had been different. This punishment was far worse. It had gone on and on. It was as if Dad wanted to hurt me over and over again. 'That can't be right,' I realised. 'He can't get away with that.'

I started to regret that I hadn't given him a flick when he'd asked. It was stupid of me not to. Even though I never enjoyed it, and sometimes my arm hurt if he took too long, it was straightforward enough.

'But he wants it all the time these days,' I thought. 'It's never-ending. And I hate doing it.'

I don't remember admitting that to myself before. I knew I didn't like what Dad made me do to him, but it was just one of those things. Events that night finally crystallised my thoughts. 'I really hate it. I wish he'd leave me alone.'

But I knew I couldn't put him off. I was a kid of fourteen. He made the rules. I'd tried saying 'no' and look where that had got me. If I could have thought of a way to make him stop, I would have taken it there and then. But there was no way out and I didn't feel that telling someone what he was doing to me was an option. For as long as I remember, he had drummed into me the threat that if I told, he would be sent to prison and I would never see him again. Although I hated what he did to me and I was beginning to realise how wrong it was, he had brainwashed me from such an early age and he was still my Dad – I didn't want to lose him.

But perhaps there *was* something? I remembered the planned trip to France. If I couldn't keep my father away from me, I could do the next best thing and take myself away from him. In my mind, Paris became my sanctuary. I would be safe there. For a while at least.

'I wish I was going tomorrow,' I thought. 'I can't wait to escape from this place.'

For the next week I could think of little else. 'I'm getting away from him,' I kept repeating to myself. 'I'm getting away.'

I was so busy looking forward to the holiday that I didn't immediately notice that I'd managed to have two baths without the dreaded knock on the door. It wasn't completely out of the ordinary – if Dad drank too much and fell asleep after dinner I could sometimes get through my ablutions and into bed before he stirred. But it was unusual. I couldn't remember when I'd last gone three or four days without seeing his penis.

At first I worried that he was punishing me for making him angry. But he seemed his normal self around the house, so that didn't make sense. But then another thought struck me. 'I don't care if he is punishing me,' I decided. 'I don't want to do it anyway. I don't want to do any of that ever again.'

The pain in my bottom took several days to disappear, and even afterwards it was never far from my thoughts. Just hearing Dad whistling around the house without a care in the world or trying to make the odd bit of conversation across the dinner table each evening brought the full horror of that night rushing back. Sometimes I physically sweated just talking to him. If he noticed, he said nothing.

A week without seeing my father's face, some respite from being reminded of the sound of his breathing on my neck, seemed like heaven. Paris couldn't come quickly enough for me.

I was desperate for a distraction from my home life. After what I'd been through, it seemed important to me to focus on relationships with people my own age – people who might be going through similar problems of their own at home. As Dad kept saying, 'Everyone does what we do. They just don't talk about it.'

What would really set the holiday off, of course, was if I got together with one of the French students. The best-looking girl on the visit to our school was called Michaela, and for some reason, completely out of keeping with my normal track record, I actually got somewhere with her. On a trip to the ice rink at Grimsby she let me hold her hand. I was so flushed, I thought I'd melt the ice. I couldn't wait until she could show me around her own country.

While the French kids were over it seemed even more important than usual to show off, and I didn't see why they shouldn't be impressed by the same things as the Lafford lot. There wasn't a boy or girl in our school who wouldn't admire you if you had the latest gadget or the fullest pack of Benson & Hedges and I needed to pull out all the stops to woo Michaela. Such things, of course, all cost money. Fortunately I had my sources.

Although Dad was still slipping me twenty B&H every couple of weeks, I needed more now there were new kids in town to impress. My occasional practice of dipping into Dad's wallet went into overdrive, and even he noticed. One night I simply could not find it anywhere. What's more, the keys to his van were nowhere to be seen either. Not to worry. There was always Plan B.

Mum's purse was always kept in the same place. Unless I was really desperate for money, it always seemed too easy to rob from her. I preferred the challenge of nicking off Dad whenever possible. Not only did he deserve it more, he had a lot more to steal. While I kept my gains from Mum to twenty pence or so in case she got suspicious, I made off with handfuls of notes from him. But this time I had no choice. There were a dozen French under-age smokers depending on me and I wasn't going to let them down.

As usual, I waited till there was no one downstairs and then took Mum's purse from her handbag and helped myself. On this occasion I was going for a couple of quid.

Just as I pulled the green notes out, I heard a voice behind me. It was Jo.

'I'm telling Mum,' she said, and before I could stop her she had left the kitchen and was flying up the stairs screaming, 'Mum! Mum! Duncan's stealing money from your purse!'

'Oh shit,' I thought, and I braced myself for the worst.

My mother came raging into the room and didn't even ask whether I had taken money or not. If Jo said it was true, that was good enough for her. For a while I thought she was going to beat me up, she was so furious. It was the mother of all tellings-off and I'll admit I was scared. But I knew it would pass. It always did.

The tirade finally ended with Mum screaming the words, 'You're grounded.'

'Thank God it's over,' I thought, and I started to walk out of the kitchen to go to my room. But it was not over. The punishment was just beginning.

'And you can forget about going to France, you nasty thief,' my mother added. 'You're not going anywhere for a month.'

The words hung in the air behind me for what seemed like ages as I struggled to digest them. Was she saying what I thought she was saying? She couldn't be. She couldn't.

But she was.

My mouth fell open and I had to fight back the tears. I didn't care who saw me. Being grounded I could normally handle – I loved our garden. But not allowed to go to Paris on the exchange trip? I wouldn't get to see Michaela. I would have to go to school with all the other losers.

And worst of all, I'd get no break from Dad.

I was stunned, rooted to the spot. A dozen thoughts swirled around my mind. It felt as if time stood still, but it must have taken less than a second. When the jumble in my head cleared, I was left with only one conclusion.

'If I can't get away, it could happen again,' I panicked. 'He could hurt me like before.'

That realisation completely knocked the wind out of me. I'd pinned my hopes on escaping my dad's clutches in Paris, on not seeing his face for a week, but until that moment I hadn't appreciated just how much I wanted to get away. How much I needed to. I felt physically sick as my mother's words sank in.

I begged and I pleaded with her, but she was adamant. 'You're not going and that's that. I don't care what your father says!'

'It's not fair!' I screamed, and I ran out the door and up to my room.

I sobbed on my bed, my head still spinning with thoughts about the ramifications. Of course I was crushed at not seeing Michaela again, but that wasn't what was making me feel like my life was draining from me. I wanted to go to France to get away from Dad. I needed to think about things without him around. I needed some respite from remembering that horrible night in the bathroom every time I saw or heard him. But Mum didn't know that. She didn't know just how important this trip was to me. Could I somehow tell her?

I knew the answer to that before I'd even thought of the question.

Of course I couldn't tell her. What would I say? 'I don't like what Dad does to me in the bathroom'?

'No,' I thought. 'I've got to do something else.'

As a former nurse, Mum had never got out of the habit of hoarding medication for any possible problem. As her access to prescription drugs dwindled over the years, her medicine cabinet basically amounted to little more than a selection of painkillers. But boy did she have a lot of them.

I went into the bathroom and poured myself a glass of water into my favourite *Ghostbusters* beaker. Then I reached into the medicine cabinet and took down Mum's drug box. In it was a bottle of 500 paracetamol, about half full. I took the water and the pills back to my bedroom, sat on the bed and started to swallow the tablets one by one. The more I swallowed, the more I cried. And the more I cried, the more I swallowed. I began to scoop handfuls from the bottle and pressed my palm over my mouth to fit as many inside as possible.

'This will teach them,' I raged silently to myself. 'Mum will never ground me again. And Dad – Dad will never touch me like that again. Never.'

After ten minutes the bottle was nearly empty. I closed my eyes and lay back on the bed.

'Never again,' I thought. 'Never again.'

10

You're a 'Page 57'

Looking back, I suppose it was a cry for help. And if it was, I guess my mother heard.

I don't know why she came up to my room. Maybe she wanted to apologise to me. Maybe she wanted to give me another piece of her mind. All I know is, she probably saved my life.

When she came into my bedroom, the first thing she would have seen is me, lying back on the bed, drifting in and out of consciousness and still half crying. Perhaps she would have noticed the empty pill bottle in my hand or possibly a couple of stray tablets on the floor. Perhaps, with her medical background, she only needed to see my prone position and the empty glass on the side table to suspect all was not well. Whatever the thought process, she quickly set about trying to put things right.

'My God, what have you done?' she screamed. But she already knew the answer. 'I must call Dr Kerr!'

In between fussing around with the phone book, Mum tried a few of her rusty medical tricks. I don't know how many are standard practice for overdose victims, but she didn't have much to work with by way of hospital supplies. Her first instinct was to make me vomit. To that end she force-fed me mustard, vinegar and water, holding my drooping head up to try to get each mouthful down my throat.

It didn't work. I was too tired to swallow. And it tasted vile.

'I can't, it's horrible,' I spluttered.

'Drink it!' Mum screamed. 'You stupid boy, Duncan, it's for your own good – drink it!'

Her next thought was to sit on me in an attempt to perform a Heimlich manoeuvre on my supine body. By now she was crying more than I was, but I was too weak to help, or to respond. I think she was at the end of her tether when the local doctor arrived.

He took just seconds to deliver his opinion. 'This boy needs an ambulance,' he barked. 'Now!'

While Dr Kerr rang ahead to alert Boston Hospital, I was bundled into an ambulance with my mother alongside me. The medics were desperate not to let me go to sleep. They kept trying to talk to me, or make me talk, but what really kept me awake were the sirens. Listening to the 'woo-woo' noises as we rattled out of the village and on to the busy A road to Boston was suddenly incredibly exciting. It was like being in a Hollywood film. I could imagine all the people outside looking at the blue flashing lights and wondering, 'Who's in there? What's wrong with him? It must be serious to have all this fuss.'

Moments later I was drifting serenely along, on some level aware of the chaos around me but immune to what it meant or what it was about. It was as though I was invulnerable. Nothing could hurt me now. It was as if I had stuck two fingers up to the world.

The film scenario continued when we arrived at the hospital. I had passed out by the time the ambulance pulled into the emergency parking bay, but I awoke to find myself being wheeled down long, bleak corridors and into an operating theatre with nurses running alongside the trolley. A room had been set up in advance, and within seconds of arriving I was dressed in a hospital gown and wired up to have my stomach pumped.

Until that point I had felt as though I were watching myself in a film. It was like being in a dream. Over the next hour I finally realised it was not a dream but a nightmare. And I was in it.

For the first time I began to question what was going on. Why was I there? What had I done? Had I really wanted to kill myself? Was I trying to punish my parents? Did I want to get away from my father that much?

The thoughts flitted in and out of my mind, and I honestly couldn't think of the answers.

While my mind wandered I remember struggling to work out what was happening to me physically. Medics were pulling me here and there, and I heard different voices shouting. Most of what was said was a blur to me, but I could make out that they were upset or worried. I wanted to ask if having my stomach rinsed would hurt me, but no words came out. In hindsight, nothing they said could have prepared me for just how painful the procedure was.

As weak as I was, I felt myself resisting as one nurse held my head while another started to feed a long tube into my mouth and down my throat. I tried to scream as it scraped the sides of my throat, but I had no control over my own body. As I looked over to the nurse tending me on my left, I couldn't help vomiting. Her legs were covered and her uniform was drenched. What did she expect, sticking that thing down my throat? At home, I could have expected a smack round the ear, or worse, for such an embarrassing crime. 'Oh my God,' I thought. 'Please don't tell Mum.' The nurse must have seen the fear in my eyes. She just wiped her front with a tissue, smiled and said, 'Don't worry about it. I've had worse. You do it again if you can.'

From my right, I heard laughing from the other nurse. 'That will teach you not to wear an apron!'

For all the pain I was in, that relaxed me.

The tube going in was just the start of the ordeal. Then they turned on the water and the flushing began.

Click. Click. Click-click-click-click. Click.

One by one, then in bursts of several at a time, each tablet that was sucked out of me landed in a small metal bowl. Click. Click.

Eventually the nurses paused. Then one said to the other, 'Again?' and the procedure was repeated.

Click. Click. Click.

Again and again they flushed me out. 'If they carry on like this they'll suck me inside out,' I thought.

'Do you think we've got them all?' one nurse asked.

'I don't know,' came the reply. 'Let's do one more.'

When they were satisfied that I was empty, the nurses did one more flush, this time using milk of magnesia, and then a final spurt with charcoal liquid. On any normal day the taste of either of these would have been enough to make me puke. By now, though, I had nothing left to bring up. I was totally drained. I'd had an enema by mouth. 'Never again,' I thought, seconds before falling asleep.

Thanks to everyone's hard work, I pulled through that night, but Mum said it was 'touch and go'. I was kept in hospital for two weeks for tests and observation. I had tubes in here, tubes in there, leads connecting to all manner of monitors, ECGs and other bleeping electronica.

The critical time with paracetamol overdoses, as the doctors knew but I did not, is the week or so following the event. Getting through the first night did not actually mean I was safe. The stomach pump had only flushed out a fraction of the danger. As a result of my actions I was a clear candidate for kidney and liver failure. The breakdown, if it happened, would be slow and painful. That is how most paracetamol overdosers die. That's how I would have gone. Poisoned by my own body shutting down.

The only visitors I had during my fortnight in hospital were Mum, of course, who only left my bedside when she was ordered out, and Dad. On one visit they gave me a home-made 'get well' card from my sister, and told me that Jo had even baked me a cake for when I got home. That really cheered me up.

It was odd, looking every day at the faces of the two people who, I realised during my convalescence, were a key part of my being there in the first place. I had wanted to escape, and had in fact only achieved the exact opposite. Every time I opened my eyes one or other of them was there. I had nowhere to hide.

I don't think it was an easy time for my parents either. They actually seemed embarrassed by all the fuss. I lost count of how many times the words 'attention seeker' were used in my earshot.

Dad looked particularly uncomfortable on every visit. He

seemed most intent on apportioning blame for the whole 'episode', as they were calling it in front of me.

'He wouldn't be here now if you hadn't grounded him,' he snarled at my mother. 'You know that, don't you?'

Of course there was more to it than that, but I pretended to be asleep. I never interfered in their arguments. Mum said nothing. That was unusual in itself, but I didn't step in to help her. What could I say? 'What Mum did was only the final straw. If you hadn't forced yourself into me in the bathroom I wouldn't have wanted to get away so badly.' I couldn't do that. I couldn't talk to them about it.

Part of the hospital's treatment focused on my mental recovery. It wasn't natural for a fourteen-year-old boy to try to commit suicide, they explained to my parents. 'We'd like him to see a child psychologist, if you agree,' a doctor said.

They couldn't really say no. However, the only reason they were being consulted was on a technicality: as a minor I needed to have my guardians present when I was being assessed by the psychologist. Apart from just following the hospital's guidelines, the logic in this was that I was more likely to feel comfortable speaking to a stranger if my family were present.

Even at that age I realised this was not going to work. Two weeks of thinking about things in hospital had led me to certain dilemmas. My head was spinning with questions. Yes, I wanted them answered. But not with Dad in the room.

The sessions were a disaster. The child psychologist acted as though he had never seen a kid in his life. He talked to Mum and Dad more than me. It was as though I weren't there.

'Why do you think he took the pills?' he asked Mum.

'Has he acted like this before?' he asked Dad.

'What about asking me?' I wanted to shout. 'He knows the answers but he's not going to tell you, is he!'

Sadly, with them in the room, neither was I.

I just sat there silently, staring at my feet, while the analysis went on above my head.

After ten minutes' chat, the psychologist reached for a book from his shelf and thumbed through it. Leaning towards me, he tapped a finger on a particular paragraph and smiled.

'Here you are, my friend,' he said. 'Just as I thought. You're a "page 57".'

And that was that. Diagnosis over. I was a 'classic case of page 57', whatever that was, and that was how he was going to treat me.

I think I went to four or five sessions with him, each one about an hour. For most of it I either sat in silence or parroted the answers he prompted with his questions. Mum seemed pleased that progress was being made. Dad seemed pleased for other reasons.

When I was finally released from hospital I had a surprise waiting for me at home.

'There you go, son,' my dad said as he wheeled a brand new bike into the lounge. 'It's the one you've been asking for. You deserve it after what you've been through.'

We both knew that he wasn't talking about the stomach pump. He was talking about the bleeding in my backside a few weeks ago and what caused it. He was talking about forcing me up against the radiator against my will. He was talking about the stupid answers he heard me give the child psychologist when what I really should have been saying was, 'That's the reason I tried to kill myself. Him over there. He attacked me.'

He was talking about everything he didn't want me to tell anyone.

So he'd bought me the bike of my dreams to buy my silence, just as he had always done. I had only just set foot in the house and I realised we were already back in the old routine. Dad would give me 'treats' and I would acquiesce to his demands in the bathroom without too much fuss. Nothing had changed. After everything that had happened, nothing had changed. Everything would be just the same. For ever.

Or would it?

I don't know where the feeling came from, but something was different. Something about me. I had changed.

Normally, when Dad handed out gifts or turned a blind eye when money disappeared, I was grateful. I only ever felt gratitude and love for him. But not this time.

I looked at my father, as he stood there proudly next to my new bike, and saw only the person who had caused me so much pain a few weeks earlier. 'You're not my hero,' I thought. 'You're not the man I've always worshipped.'

I looked at the bike more closely. I treated it as an item in a shop window and not the generous gift from a loved one. With this in mind, I realised it was not in fact the one I had asked for so many times. I wanted a racing bike with five-speed derailleur gears. This one might have had drop-handlebars but the similarities ended there. And it only had three gears. Even Jo's bike had three gears.

Dad wanted to keep me quiet and maybe ease his con-science a little bit, but as far as I was concerned at that moment, he couldn't even get that right. I know I should have been grateful, and normally I would have been. Normally it would have been enough that Dad had thought to get me a present. But not any more. Not this time. I just couldn't muster the strength, and Dad knew it. No sooner had he handed over the bike than he scarpered 'to do some business'.

I suddenly realised how lonely I was. Mum hadn't told anyone why I was in hospital, and I think she had encouraged people not to visit. As a result, I hadn't seen any of my mates for weeks. I couldn't wait to put that right.

I thought about the future. It was only a matter of time before Dad came into the bathroom again while I was in there. Only a matter of time before he asked me for a 'flick' as calmly as though nothing had happened. Just as he had done so casually after the Geoff Capes motel weekend.

But it was different then. I was different. I had wanted to please him more than anything else in the world. But now? 'I'm not sure I really even like him at the moment,' I thought. 'It's going to be worse than ever.'

I spent the rest of the day torturing myself with worry about how I would respond the next time. How I would get through it, how I would react. How I would feel towards him.

I never got the opportunity to find out. From the day I came out of hospital, my father never abused me again.

I was free. I just didn't know it.

11

I Had Suffered Enough

After I came out of hospital I had a week off before going back to school. This was fine by me. I could see my friends when they came out of lessons.

For my first day of recuperation I just had my mother for company. In the face of her 'attention seeker' comments at the hospital, it was easy for me to forget that I had put her through hell. It was only when I returned home and I noticed that all medicines and tablets had disappeared from the bathroom cabinets that it sank in how worried she was. In fact, all bleach and other toxic cleaning fluid seemed to be missing from the kitchen as well. Mum was obviously terrified that I would try something like the overdose again, which made me sad that I'd put her through so much. I wanted to tell her, 'You gave me the excuse, Mum, but you weren't the reason I did it.'

As I suspected, my mother hadn't told a soul about what exactly I was in hospital for. While there was a chance I wouldn't recover, she wanted to keep things within the family. Once I was out, however, that changed.

The day after I was signed out from the hospital Mum and Dad took me to the paper shop to apologise for not doing my round over the last few weeks and to ask if my job was still available. Mum got the ball rolling by telling them about the overdose – the official line was that I had sulked about being grounded – and then it was my turn. Luckily the owners, Mr and Mrs Brierly, were nice folk and didn't let my apology go on very long. 'The important thing is that you're all right, Duncan,' they said. 'The job is still yours as soon as you want it.'

I was packed off upstairs to play computer games with Paul, the Brierlys' son, and Andrew Bembridge, a lad who had covered my round, while the adults talked for an hour or so. We had just finished the first game when one of the boys asked: 'Why did you do it?' I thought about the question for a few seconds. Now was my chance to tell someone my own age the truth. All I had to do was say the words.

I couldn't do it.

I told them instead about being grounded from the French trip. 'There's this girl I fancied,' I explained. 'It was the only way to make my mum change her mind.'

I think they thought it was cool. I thought, if they ever had to go through a stomach pump they'd soon change their minds.

By the time I got back to school the following Monday, the story had already done the rounds. In fact, it seemed to have spread all over the village. Everyone seemed to know that I had been caught stealing and had tried to commit suicide rather than face my punishment.

Complete strangers would stop Mum in the street and talk to her as though I wasn't there. 'How's Duncan?' they'd ask. 'I heard all about it. It must have been horrible for you.'

Mum, although kind and caring during my convalescence,

let me know more than once what an inconvenience it had all been for the family, especially as both she and Dad had had to take time off work. But for a while I think she enjoyed being the centre of attention.

On one occasion I was spotted cycling by the village's other GP, Dr Duke-Cox. Although Dr Kerr had helped save my life after the overdose, this was the chap I preferred to be treated by. He was funny and friendly and always spoke directly to me, instead of using my parents as an interpreter like a lot of adults. When he called me over, I went happily.

I hadn't seen him since I had left the hospital, and as I approached I started to think about what I would say. In Dr Duke-Cox I saw an opportunity. 'This is it,' I promised myself. 'When he asks why I did it, I'm going to tell him the truth.'

I was quite excited by what I was about to do. But I never got to say those words. In fact, I never got a chance to say much at all.

As soon as I was within speaking distance, the doctor said, 'You stupid little bastard. What on Earth did you do that for? You scared your mother half to death.'

I was completely taken aback. All thoughts of my hastily prepared speech tumbled from my head. Instead I trotted out the usual story. That was what he wanted to hear, after all.

The strange thing was, I think it was what I wanted to hear as well. I'd rather believe that version of events than the reality. So that was the story I told everyone, even my best mates. After a while it became second nature. Tell the same lie enough times and you begin to believe it. Almost.

In general, other kids thought what I'd been through was pretty exciting, but I don't think any adults were impressed.

My reputation in the village, if I had one, plummeted. I was the boy who had selfishly tried to worry his parents because he couldn't get his own way. I was the boy who had tried to steal from his own mother and been too cowardly to face the consequences.

People's opinion of me didn't get any better when my mother suddenly announced that, after due consideration and discussion with my father, perhaps if it wasn't too late I would be allowed to go on the trip after all.

I couldn't believe what I was hearing.

On the surface I was overjoyed. But inside I was distraught. 'All of this could have been avoided,' I thought. 'I went through all this for nothing?'

To strangers it just looked as if my 'attention seeking' had succeeded. I had bullied my parents and got my way. I wasn't a very nice boy.

As it turned out, the trip wasn't a great success. My host family lived on a farm and I was expected to help furnish the pigsties with bales of hay after breakfast. And I never managed to get a moment to myself with Michaela. But at least I was out of Billinghay and away from my father.

I had hoped the exchange trip to France would have put some distance between the past and the future in my mind. I hoped I would begin to think about my father as fondly as I used to. I wanted to want to make him happy again and not be intimidated by the thought of his touch. An episode shortly after I returned proved I still had some healing to do.

We had finished dinner and I was taking a bath. Half-way through washing myself I heard a knock on the door. I froze.

'Oh my God,' I thought. 'It's him!'

I had a sudden flashback to the events of four weeks earlier in the same room, and the identical feelings of pain and sickness that I had felt for days afterwards swamped me again now.

I couldn't help it. I was terrified. I vomited straight into my own bath-water. Tears began to stream from my eyes.

I heard another knock, and then a voice called out. It took me a few seconds to realise it wasn't his. It was my mum.

'Duncan, if you need a towel, take a fresh one from the cupboard,' she said.

Never in my life have I been so happy to hear my mother's voice.

I realised then that I still wasn't over what had driven me to the paracetamol in the first place. The thought of my father subjecting me to anything like it again made me physically quake.

I decided to keep a low profile where Dad was concerned. If he couldn't see me, I reasoned, he wouldn't think of touching me. Out of sight, out of mind.

After a couple of weeks of strategically getting home long after I knew he would have eaten and crashed out on the sofa, my plan of avoidance was going well. Too well, it seemed. Something odd was happening. And then I realised: my father was doing his best to stay out of my way as well.

For some reason this bothered me in a way I couldn't understand. 'What's he up to?' I wondered. I didn't know, but I decided to make the most of the freedom it gave me.

For a while I was happy to be left to my own devices, relieved that I could finally take a bath without having anyone else in the room demanding my attention. I still had the porn my father gave me, I still watched the videos he'd put in my room. But, for the first time in as long as I could remember, I didn't have to do anything in return.

And that was when it hit me. As much as I'd hated the physical assaults and the wearying sessions making him come, I'd grown attached to the time we spent together. There were never any other people involved. It was just us two, father and son, alone with each other.

That's why it bothered me that he was avoiding me now.

The fact that Dad always said 'This is our little secret' just made it more special. No one else shared my father's time like this. No one else gave him this much pleasure. No one else meant as much to him as me. I was truly proud and happy that he loved me so much.

'Is it all over now?' I wondered. 'Have I ruined everything?'

Where were the special times we shared? Where was the sense of camaraderie, the secret bond that linked us? Where were the winks when he covered for me in front of Mum, the packets of B&H once a month, the ridiculous amount of pound notes left where I could have them away? Where were the unexpected gifts after a particularly fraught flick session? Where was the closeness?

'It must be because of the suicide attempt,' I thought. 'It's my fault. I've made him unhappy. He's punishing me.' He had told me enough times that this is what fathers did if they loved their sons, so now that he wasn't doing it to me any more, there was only one conclusion: he didn't love me.

The more I thought about our relationship, the sadder I felt. 'It's like I don't exist any more,' I thought. 'The bastard's cut me out of his life.'

Where before I literally couldn't take a piss without him sneaking up on me, wanting to talk to me about sex, about what I was up to at school, about my friends, now I was honoured if he stepped into the house while I was home. It was as if he was actually trying to deprive me of his company, to excise me from his life altogether. And it hurt.

I realised how much I missed him.

While I felt ostracised from my father, my relationship with my mother seemed to be deteriorating fast. The warm bond which I'd felt between us while I recuperated from the overdose seemed well and truly gone. By the time I returned from France, we were incapable of communicating for more than a few minutes without it becoming a fight.

I could see it happening, but I was at a loss to understand why, or to prevent it. I don't know whether the time away from home had made me even more frustrated by my mother's iron rule, or whether I was still fuming at being first told I could go, then I couldn't, then finally I could.

Looking back, I suspect we were both handling the distant behaviour of my father in the same way: badly.

On one occasion I swore at her and she slapped my face. For a moment we stood staring at each other. Then I said, 'Do it again. I dare you.'

She walked away.

At the time I was exhilarated by the confrontation, but I soon realised I was channelling my anger towards the wrong person. My mum was there, she was convenient, so she took the brunt of my frustration.

Looking back, I think it must have been the same for her.

My dad wasn't much help around the house at the best of times. For the last couple of months he'd been virtually invisible. After so many years of marriage, I get the feeling

he knew how to play my mother to get out of tricky conversations. If he found himself out of his depth in a discussion,
he knew exactly which buttons to press to goad her into a
convenient rage. Discussion over.

Like Mum, I was quick to raise my voice. But where
important topics were concerned I employed avoidance tactics. I guess I got that from my dad.

After a few weeks of the silent treatment, the atmosphere
between me and my father started to soften. I sensed a definite
shift in both our attitudes, unspoken as usual – just as the
original problem was never discussed.

Gradually he started to open up a bit more, and I noticed
him once again beginning to stick up for me against Mum
when she was angry with me. For my part, despite the fear
that I might be called upon to give Dad a flick, I found myself
not rushing to my room whenever I heard his van pull up
outside the house, although being alone in his company still
filled me with unease. As much as I'd missed the attention, I
couldn't shake the fear that he might want another flick. I also
didn't like being confronted by the questions that slipped into
my head every time I saw him. What if my suspicions were
right? The only way to cope was to ignore the problem, by
whatever means possible.

Dad also started taking me to his work unit once again, and
out on deliveries. Maybe he just wanted to 'keep up appearances', but I appreciated the gestures. I had not enjoyed being
scared of him. I really had missed him.

For all I knew, another bathroom episode was just around
the corner, but I'd deal with that when it happened. For the
moment we were doing all right without it, as long as I kept
my doubts under control. At Dad's request I still delivered

porn to my teacher and brought videos back, although not so often. There were always dirty magazines in Dad's truck or around his office, and he encouraged me to browse through them. 'What do you think of her then?' he would ask. 'Which are the best tits on that page?' At home this often used to be the preamble to a flick. But out of the house it seemed more superficial, more innocent. Every time it didn't lead any further I let out a sigh of relief. It was as if he wanted us to become 'mates'. I was still as confused as hell, but that was a start. 'Mates' didn't hurt each other in the bathroom. I'd settle for that for now.

If I could stop having nightmares about him penetrating me, life would be near perfect.

Throughout the weeks from my overdose to recovery, Johanna remained very quiet. She had been openly pleased to see me when I came home from hospital, and was visibly relieved to discover I was going to be OK. Even her promised cake was as delicious as Mum had predicted.

But then, as things began to settle back to normal, she had drifted into the background. I didn't appreciate it at first, but from that day on she stopped trying to get me into trouble. She even turned the occasional blind eye to some of my later indiscretions. Did she feel guilty about her part in my suicide attempt, I wondered. If so, she shouldn't have. It wasn't her fault.

Whatever the reason, it was clear that she felt I had suffered enough.

12

Just One Cornetto

My father may not have subscribed to the 'money can't buy me love' school of thought, but he believed a free chicken could go a long way in the right direction. If there was a person in the village he wanted to impress, he would break off talking to them, walk round the back of his van and reappear a few moments later clutching a couple of frozen birds. He liked to be seen as generous. In Dad's mind generosity equated with success. It was a trait I would naturally pick up and replicate in my own dealings with people later.

My friends were also targets for Dad to impress. The catapults and airguns and cigarettes and booze he bought me always found themselves in my mates' hands eventually, and he knew it. Everyone had cause to like him, although Andy got the biggest treat.

'Fancy a ride on the ferry?' Dad asked me one day. 'I've got a bit of business in Holland. You can bring a mate.'

And so it was that Andy, Dad and I ended up in Amsterdam one spring morning. I admit that at the time I was a little peeved that none of my friends visited me while I was in hospital, but once I learned that Mum had asked them not to, I forgot the matter, so it was great to see Andy again. As for my father, I was looking forward to seeing what 'business' he had lined up in the land of clogs and tulips, but we never got to find out. No sooner had the bus dropped us in the centre of the city than Dad stuffed a few guilders in my pocket and said, 'I'll see you back here at six. And don't be late.'

The last we saw of him was as he crossed the bridge towards the area's famous Red Light District.

'Do you think he's going after a hooker?' Andy asked me.

I shrugged. Anything was possible with my dad. I had no idea what he was up to, but my stomach started churning with worry anyway. I was sure that whatever 'business' it was wouldn't meet with my mother's approval. The guilders in my hand were to ensure she never found out.

Although I didn't know what my father was up to, I knew one thing for certain: he was lying. One liar can always spot another.

Even though Dad hadn't confided in me, I still felt uncomfortable about sharing my fears with Andy. But by covering up for him, I was inadvertently lying to my closest friend yet again, as I had done so many times in the past. I couldn't help it. Yet again my father was making me drive a wedge between myself and my mates. I was being forced to side with him whether I wanted to or not. It had happened so often before, but this time was different. This time I knew it was wrong.

'What sort of "mate" puts you in this kind of position?' I asked myself. The sort, I realised, who was more interested in his own pleasure than anyone else's feelings, and to hell with the consequences. 'He hasn't changed at all. He's just the same as he always was.'

My father had tricked me into silence yet again. I promised myself it would be the last time.

The poultry business seemed to be going so well for Dad that his accountant advised him to 'go limited'. Dad opted not to, but that didn't stop him buying new vehicles, as well as a warehouse out on the main road into Billinghay, and employing quite a few of my mates to do odd jobs around his yard. Whenever I cycled past his place or stopped off to help at weekends, there would be someone I knew, either by name or by sight, from the lower years at school, cleaning his vans or carrying boxes.

Even my mother got roped in to do the bookkeeping, and for a while we were a family business. The harmony didn't last long. I think Mum spotted a few too many irregularities in the figures, and they began to argue even more than usual. Some of the questions Mum was throwing at him Dad struggled to answer; others he just refused point-blank to discuss. Exit Mum.

She was replaced by Andy's mother, Janice, which I wasn't happy with at all. Keeping track of a few receipts was a piece of cake for someone as smart as Janice, and I guess she could do with the few extra pounds a week. But I hated playing at Andy's from then on, knowing Dad could drop by any moment with invoices or questions he didn't want to ask on the telephone. Andy's place had been my sanctuary for years, and now he was invading it.

Andy's house was huge, with four floors and a basement. Because of its size and the relaxed attitude of his mum, we had many a sleepover at his place. We would sit up late listening to music, looking out of the window with his telescope or even going for walks down the riverbank. The best thing was that we didn't have a curfew when we were there. 'Who can they piss off walking along a riverbank?' appeared to be Janice's logic. She was right. More often than not we would play MERP, and sometimes drink a beer or sniff gas.

During summer we were allowed to stray further. One evening, Andy, Stephen and I – the usual suspects – were out for a late-night wander, killing time for no reason at all as normal, when we found ourselves by the dyke that went up one side of the school grounds. A few hundred yards away was the open-air swimming pool, now shimmering in the moonlight. Attracted like moths to the light shining from the pool building, we climbed over the chicken wire that marked the boundaries of the school grounds, then shinned up and over the wooden slat fence inside. Why did we do it? For the same reason we did anything: boredom. But as soon as we got up to the water's edge, it was obvious what had to be done. I can't remember who went first, but within minutes we were all stripped off and lowering ourselves into the water.

It was heaven. And it was our secret.

We kept as quiet as we could, speaking in whispers and being careful not to splash around. The last thing we needed was for some early riser to hear us and spoil our bliss. We stayed in the pool until the horizon began to change to a lighter shade of blue, then we got out, put our clothes on to our wet bodies and walked back to Andy's house with our secret.

That summer we went back to the pool on many occasions. Sometimes there would be a cover over it, sometimes not. Sometimes the light would be on; at other times we skinny-dipped in darkness. It was as close to perfection as any of us could imagine. 'What could be better than this?' we asked each other every time.

With hindsight, the answer is obvious: girls.

None of us was particularly cool, not without cigarettes to barter, and we all took contact with girls where we could. We weren't what you would call 'initiators'. But of course there were girls who would have run to join in our secret swimming sessions. I kicked myself later for not realising it at the time, but out of Annie, Cheryl, Trisha, Justine and even the fabled Tracey Black, surely at least a couple of them would have been up for a no-strings-attached swim? The chance of seeing any of those young ladies wet, naked and bathed in moonlight would have been worth the risk of being grassed up by them if they turned us down. But we'll never know. At the time, we were too stupid to find out.

'Stupidity' was an accusation I was starting to have levelled at me at school. My grades were slipping each term and my record for handing in homework was getting worse. The problem with homework, of course, is that it needs to be done outside school hours. Since most of my time after five o'clock was spent either high on glue or playing with my mates – or both – I didn't devote much time to study. In my mind it was another thing that I associated with being at home. And home was the last place I ever wanted to be.

While mother and I were still locking horns, my relationship with my father was on something like an even keel, but there was still the fear that he could hurt me again at any time. He wasn't ignoring me any more, which meant more to me than I could understand, but that didn't mean I wanted to spend time with him. Just seeing my dad reminded me of the questions swarming around my head: about the things he made me do, and about the differences between him and a paedophile. Sometimes it was easier not to think about things.

My distraction policy at home spread to school, and I started to pay less attention during classes. The highlight of our maths lesson was often a game called 'grope poker'. As its name suggests, it had nothing to do with arithmetic – and everything to do with getting close to Tracey Black.

The game involved six people, who all sat together, including me, Tracey, Mark Steele and Susan Temple. The rules were simple; the object even more obvious. You had to roll one die to see who was 'it' and another to see what you groped for ten seconds. There was one list of body parts for girls and another for boys, and it wasn't uncommon for me to end up groping one of the lads or Susan's shoulder. Despite the instinctive fear of a male's touch that had terrified me during the sleepover with Andy, somehow this seemed a gamble worth risking. It might be Mark's arse this time, but on the next go you could hit the jackpot and be invited to touch the holy grail of grope poker: Tracey's breasts.

I had more fun in my maths class in the following – my final – year. Once again, it was indirectly as a result of my home life. Despite what had happened before, I was still helping myself to cash from Mum's purse and Dad's wallet. Fifty pence here, a couple of quid there. Even if they realised, they were turning a blind eye. Nobody wanted a repeat of last time. Getting shopkeepers to sell me cigarettes was no problem either. 'They're for my mum,' I would say, and since they knew Mrs Fairhurst got through about sixty a day, they handed them over.

There were several places in the school grounds where you could smoke out of sight of the teachers. A girl called Alison

Cosby hung out with one group, I hung out with another. Every so often there was crossover between the groups when a sort of cultural exchange took place, and this always took place during Mr Bridgewater's maths class. In the beginning Alison would let me feel her breasts for a cigarette. It had to be Embassy No. 1, though; none of the corner shop's own brand. Usually I was only able to manage a quick squeeze through her blouse when the teacher wasn't looking. Things got a little hotter once when I gave her a pack of ten; to my amazement she faked being asleep over her desk and encouraged me to undo her bra, so I was able to slip inside and cup her naked flesh. I think I even managed to do the bra up again before I continued with my work.

The thrill was unbelievable. Not only was there the very real prospect of being caught by the teacher, but I experienced physical sensations that left me in no doubt about how I felt about girls. Every fibre of my body seemed to respond with every touch. Sometimes just the thought of brushing against the girl of my dreams was enough to provoke the same reaction, the same butterfly stomach, the same breathless recklessness. By contrast, I had played enough grope poker to know that boys' bodies held no interest for me. On the contrary, they made me feel distinctly uncomfortable, although I would touch them as a stepping-stone to a girl. Other lads seemed happy to horse around naked in the communal showers after PE lessons, gesturing to someone's physical appearance, sometimes even grappling each other in innocent high jinks. But not me.

I was never comfortable in the company of naked males. The hundreds of times I had been undressed with my father prevented that. I don't think that at fourteen I put two and two together, but looking back the connection is obvious. At the time I viewed other males with a suspicion I couldn't articulate. It was as if I had a subconscious fear they would touch me in the way my father so often had. His words 'This is how fathers love their sons' echoed in my head. What if my friends showed their love in the same way?

Each time the thought entered my head I swatted it away. Girls were my focus. Only girls.

Ali in my class liked me a bit, but I was too immature to realise it. She arranged for her father to teach me to ride a motorbike. He never suspected what we got up to.

Of all the girls in the village I think Trisha liked me the most. A play fight on the field led to a bit of groping on my account, which I interpreted as her love for me. I think now that if I had had the courage to ask her out, she would have accepted. But, as usual, I didn't.

I know I wasn't the only kid whose experience with girls began and ended with rough-and-tumble fumblings after school, but I seemed to be more uptight about it than the others. I had been raised to accept that people you love will let you touch them and will do things to your body. The only condition was that you didn't discuss it. Yet the other boys were very open about what they got up to with girls, which confused me.

I was much more comfortable handing over an Embassy No. 1 in exchange for a brief frisson of delight as I stroked a clothed breast. I'd had ten years of being given treats in return for giving my dad a flick. That was the way of the world as far as I was concerned. 'I've got something she wants, she's got something I want,' I used to think. 'Let's do business.' I never stopped to think that some things shouldn't be seen simply as cold transactions. I never stopped to question whether my sexual exploration was worth more than the same emotions I had when I swapped football stickers in the playground. Ten years of flicks for treats had done that, I suppose. Ten years of being taught to see sexual favours as a commodity.

I can't put my finger on when I finally admitted that Dad's behaviour with me was 'sexual'. I tried to deny the realisation for so long that I'm not sure when it actually broke through into my thoughts. But it was a suspicion I had held for too long. Friends' claims that 'queers suck cock' and 'gays take it up the arse' could only stay suppressed for a finite amount of time. I gradually admitted that I was guilty of all of the above. And more. And if that was true, as innocent as I believed I was, it was actual 'sex'. I could dress it up however I wanted but, at the end of the day, I had been having sex with my father.

Or he had with me.

'Is there a difference?' I asked myself. 'Does that make me gay?'

I knew the answer was 'no'. I also knew that Dad wasn't gay either. 'He's married with two kids,' I reasoned. So there must be some middle ground, I decided. There must be some sort of sex that families do that's different to the stuff lovers get up to.

I had to believe that. I had to believe that I wasn't different from anyone else. Even though I was relieved on a daily basis that Dad seemed to have stopped knocking on the bathroom door when I was inside, I had to believe that we were normal. Even though I couldn't get through a week without sniffing gas or glue to help me block out the fear I still felt when I was alone in the house with my father, I had to believe I wasn't the only one going through it. 'It's the same for everybody,' I repeated to myself.

I soon had the chance to objectify another woman. What could be more normal than that?

The most memorable girl from my school days was definitely Kelly McVitie. She was also a gas sniffer, although she came into it from a different angle to me. One sunny Sunday afternoon a whole group of us were walking from the swimming pool to the playing fields. Kelly had to go back to her house for some reason. I offered to keep her company. There was no ulterior motive on my part. I didn't fancy her. I was just being nice.

We went into her house and chatted for a bit. Kelly made me a cup of tea, switched on the TV and said, 'I won't be long, OK?'

'Sure,' I said, and she disappeared upstairs. I finished my cuppa, watched some kids' programme and realised that I wanted to pee. Kelly had been gone a while, so I figured that if she had taken a shower she would have been well finished. I knew the toilet was up a few stairs, then round a corner to the right. I stood up, went up the steps, turned the bend and then every thought of needing a piss vanished instantly from my mind.

At the top of the stairs was a full-length dress mirror. Because of the angles, I could see into Kelly's room and could see her wrapped in a towel, combing her wet hair. I was rooted to the spot, I couldn't move. She seemed to comb her hair for ages. Either that or time suddenly slowed way down. Eventually she finished her hair, stood up to remove her towel and stepped out of view.

It was just a few seconds, but in that time I saw perfection standing before me.

It was just a few seconds, but I wanted more.

What did I do? Did I call out, 'Kels, where's the bog?' Did I go back into the front room to wait out the time before she came downstairs? No. I crept up the rest of the stairs as slow as you like, hoping above hope that they wouldn't creak and give the game away.

Thanks to the angle of the mirror I didn't have to go far. Very soon I was greeted with an image straight out of every teenage boy's fantasies. As I stared, open-mouthed and with brain on autopilot, I wondered, 'How come I have never noticed this goddess before?' She was obviously the most beautiful thing in the world. Was it the small facial scar that had stopped me from noticing the rest of her? Kids are like that, aren't they? Especially mid-teenagers. The smallest imperfection and that's it. Was it because she kept herself to herself most of the time?

Whatever the reason, I had noticed her now.

She stood there naked, this time with a small hairbrush, standing straight, arms reaching up and behind to brush her hair. I will remember that image till the day I die.

After what seemed like an eternity she started to walk around the room doing other things, and kept going out of my view. I couldn't control myself now. I was acting totally on instinct. I crept to the top of the stairs, and sat directly outside her door to get a clear view into her room.

Kelly was walking around her bed carrying a pair of panties in her left hand. For a second she cast a glance towards the door and instead of screaming, she smiled. I smiled back and stood up.

At least that's what I thought had happened.

In reality she hadn't seen me at all. Whatever was making

the edges of her mouth curl up, it wasn't the sight of me hovering like an imbecile outside her door. I know this because in the next second she did see me. And this time she really did scream.

'Oops,' I mumbled. 'Sorry, I needed a piss.'

I don't know if she heard me. The door slammed in my face at the same time.

I went to the toilet, then trotted downstairs to await her fully-dressed reaction. I'd never received a bollocking from someone my own age before. That was about to change.

'What the fuck were you doing, you idiot?' she shouted at me. 'You really freaked me out. Don't ever do shit like that again!'

'Sorry,' I spluttered. 'I needed the loo. I couldn't hold it.'

It sounded pathetic and, as stories go, it was. The only consolation was that Kelly hadn't realised just how long I'd been marvelling at her. If she had, that would have been the end of our friendship. Another person I'd casually told lies to without thinking of their own feelings, just as I had done so often to Andy, Stephen and Jim. Another person whose friendship was at risk due to my increasing inability to treat people as something other than pawns in my own chess game.

I sometimes wonder what would have happened if instead of lying I'd said, 'You're the most beautiful girl I've ever seen, Kelly. I couldn't resist watching you.' Maybe she would have told me to get lost. Or perhaps she would have been flattered by my openness and invited me into her room.

It's pointless to speculate about what might have been. I wasn't the sort of person who could deal with emotions and matters of sexual interest directly. Looking back, I'm not surprised. I didn't recognise a pattern at the time, but if my father could coerce me into revealing my body to him with a few kind words and some special treats, why wouldn't I assume others could be won over by the same tactics? If I'm honest, I don't think I saw Kelly as a person. She was a girl with a fine body. Once I'd noticed that, it was almost as though Kelly the person had ceased to exist.

Was it instinct, or was I copying the behaviour of my father?

One thing was certain: I knew lying would always get me out of trouble. After so much practice, it was almost second nature to me. I lied to my parents, I lied to Kelly, and I lied to my friends. I'd been doing it for so long I didn't even register myself doing it any more. Originally it was a defence mechanism to cover up my home life and what I was up to with my father. But that had stopped a while ago. So why was I still lying?

What was I afraid of?

Cigarettes and other playground currency might have won me kudos with the majority of the kids at school, but I was very aware that it was a temporary acceptance. The reason I hung around with my own gang so much was because we all had something in common. We were all outsiders. Me, Jim, Stephen and Andy were all born outside the village. It's not as if we were from another country or our skin was a different colour, but it was enough for the other kids not to like us. We were 'different' in their eyes. As I said, it wasn't a view they held consistently, depending on what we had to offer. But it was always there, in the background.

We were a tight-knit group – both before and after Jim

eventually drifted away from our set-up. We did everything together. We played MERP together, drank booze together, sniffed glue together and inhaled gas together. And we smoked cannabis together.

It was Andy who gave me my first spliff. He said he'd got it from his brother, but I suspect he had stolen it from his mother.

Everyone knew about Andy's parents smoking dope. One of the first things we heard when we moved to Billinghay was how they'd been arrested for growing their own weed in the garden. The same thing happened to my friend Alan Kidd's dad. He was busted with eight-foot plants towering over the six-foot fence around their house!

Andy's dad died long before I met the family. It affected the whole family really badly, and perhaps that explains his mum's laid-back attitude to life as far as us kids were concerned.

It was Janice who first discovered we were sniffing glue. There were so many adverts on the television telling parents about the dangers of glue-sniffing, and what to look out for in your kids, that it was only a matter of time before one of us was caught. Most mums and dads put the spots around the mouth, mood swings and general lethargy down to just being a teenager with normal acne, but Andy's mother was more savvy than that. As usual, she handled it in a way we could only respect.

'I don't want you using glue or gas any more,' she told Andy. 'It'll kill you. I'm not losing you.'

Andy hung his head in shame. But his mum hadn't finished.

'If you want to get high, use dope,' she said, and she handed over some cannabis.

As a tactic it worked. Once we established a supply of dope, we never touched gas or glue again.

The thing that made Janice stand out for us was that she treated us like adults. She felt that some problems couldn't be solved by talking, not at first anyway. Some issues just had to be forgotten. And getting high – whether you needed to forget the pain of being molested or just of feeling insignificant – made everything seem all right.

My first dope experience stays with me today. Andy and I were walking along the banks of the River Skirth, near to his house. It was really only a dyke, but to us it was the Nile or Amazon because of the adventures and opportunities if offered.

Not far from the house was an old sewage-works. We sometimes used to break in and sit either side of the giant piston arms that powered the plant. It was ridiculously dangerous and it smelled awful, but it was another hiding-place for us where we could forget our real lives.

We had smoked hemp seeds before with no result. 'You don't know what you're doing,' Andy would say. And he was right.

This time, however, he produced a small piece of squidgy black hash and said, 'Do you want a smoke of this?'

I sat in awe as he rolled a spliff. He had obviously done it before, because it was very neat. When I attempted it, Andy laughed and started singing, 'Just one Cornetto . . .' It was, I admit, more of a cone than a tube.

The hit from the hash was very nice and very powerful. For a while we spaced out on the stones outside the sewage-works. Then Andy said he had the 'munchies' and suggested we go back to his house for a drink. When we got there we had a mug of tea and devoured a whole packet of Rich Tea biscuits.

'I can get used to this,' I said. 'Glue can kill you, but this stuff just makes you want to dunk biscuits. Result!'

I spoke too soon. Ten minutes later I was running to the toilet in order to throw up. It was an odd sensation. I didn't feel ill, I just had this irresistible urge to vomit. Kneeling over the pan, I heaved five times and watched five solid lumps of Rich Tea come back up and out.

Still not back on Planet Earth, Andy stood in the doorway and watched. 'You're spewing up little mice,' he laughed. And I could see his point. The lumps did look odd. A swig of mouthwash later and I followed my friend into his room to listen to music. 'You can't imagine how good this stuff sounds when you're stoned,' he said. And, yet again, he was right.

Cannabis proved to be a great way to forget the present and completely obliterate the past. It didn't have much effect on the future, though, and as June 1986 approached I wondered what was to become of me. My sister Johanna had signed up for college straight from school and then went on to do three years' training to be a nurse – just as Mum had done a couple of decades earlier. Jo didn't contribute financially to the household in those years. That wasn't an option for me. From the moment I left school, aged fifteen, I was expected to pay my way.

For a while when I was a kid I dreamed of becoming a policeman. Mum's memories of her own father's career painted an attractive picture of the force. Then I'd fantasised about becoming a vet like James Herriot. But ever since that trip to the Royal Signals regiment in Dorset when I was thirteen, whenever I pictured myself as an adult it was wearing a military uniform.

I was lucky in 1985 that our school arranged a visit from the army as part of the careers advice programme for those of us about to leave. Jim and I were eager to learn as much from the guest soldiers as possible, and a decent queue formed behind us in the hall while we fired question after question at the patient squaddies.

I don't know what made me ask one final question, but I wish now I hadn't. The answer to that particular query was not what I wanted to hear at all.

'I don't suppose it matters if you've got a police record?' I asked innocently. 'Soldiers must get up to all sorts.'

'You must be joking, son,' the soldier replied. 'Only clean slates get anywhere near this outfit. You haven't been a naughty boy by any chance, have you?'

Of course I had. Both Jim and I had cautions coming out our ears. Nothing major, but as juvenile criminal records go, our pasts made interesting reading: receiving stolen goods, possession of ammunition, vandalism . . .

So that was it. Because of our police form we were stuffed. The army wouldn't touch us with a bayonet.

'Fuck, fuck, fuck!' I thought. 'That's it. I'm stuck here, stuck in this fucking dump with my parents. Fuck!'

Years later I learned that my juvenile record wouldn't have mattered. I may have had a royal flush of cautions but I'd never been put away for anything. As far as the army was concerned, I had a clean bill of health.

But I didn't know that then. I didn't know anything except that my dreams had been stolen from me. My 'escape route' from Billinghay had been closed off. I was going nowhere. Literally.

I walked home from school that day struggling to fight back

the tears. Dad was reading a newspaper at the dining table when I arrived and told him about my disappointment. I don't know what I expected him to say. 'Hard luck, son' or 'They don't know what they're missing' would have been nice. What I got instead was like a kick in the stomach.

Barely lifting his head up from the paper, he said, 'I'm not surprised. You've only got yourself to blame. You've become a real loser of late.'

Thanks, Dad.

I'd been trying my best to get on with him ever since my overdose, and this was how he treated me. I was crushed. It seemed so out of the blue. He wouldn't have said that a few years ago. Not when he could get something from me.

But being snubbed by my father wasn't the worst of it. If this was what he thought, I knew that Mum's opinion would be even harsher. That's just how it was. 'I'm fucked,' I thought. 'I may as well give up now.'

My ambitions changed yet again that evening. As soon as I left school I was going to dedicate my life to getting high as often as I could and by any means possible. Glue and gas had been there for me when I was trying to block out my father's advances a couple of years ago. Substance abuse had helped me through some difficult times with my friends. Now I needed chemical help again. And if I never set foot in the reality of my parents' world again, all the better.

'That'll show the fuckers,' I thought. 'I don't need them.'

13

I Thought it Was Over

While I was at school, my reports always said the same thing: 'Could do better'. Sometimes I think they wrote it automatically as soon as they saw my name. There was a time when I scored 98 per cent in one report but the teacher still wrote the same summation: 'Could do better'. That was when I lost faith in the whole educational system.

There was never a thought that I might want to, or be able to, continue my education after school. That was the increasing view of my parents and it was rubber-stamped by the teachers at the Lafford. Since I'd got back from the French trip, I had become the typical 'black sheep'. I could barely speak to my mother without us arguing, and I had plummeted down the class tables at school. I was hardly a good prospect. 'What is the point of wasting more government money on trying to drum some knowledge into his head?' seemed to be the stance of the school. The opinion from home was even more telling: 'What is the point of wasting more of our money on that useless layabout when he could be out earning a crust?'

So it was that I was signed up for a Youth Training Scheme. I had to learn a trade. I had to earn a few pounds. I had to contribute to the household.

My first YTS placement was at an outdoor pursuits centre in Belford, Northumberland. Rather than being farmed out to a private contractor, I was actually working for the YTS itself. They used the Windy Gyle in Belford as a team-building place, and so I spent a couple of weeks learning orienteering, rock climbing and canoeing. The plan was to prepare candidates for the outside world, but, along with a girl on the course, I fell in love with what we got up to there and we requested to be given permanent jobs at the Windy Gyle, helping others to train. 'What a great scheme that would be,' I thought.

Luckily for us, the centre agreed and we were signed up for a month's trial. The centre liked us, we got on well with the staff, and we pretty much broke our backs trying to be as helpful as possible. It was all going so well, and then we were offered the terms of employment: the centre said we could each have a two-year apprenticeship on condition that we were able to provide some basic equipment of our own – a climbing harness, climbing shoes, safety helmet and a few other bits and bobs. We were both skint. The YTS refused to fund it, as did our parents, and so that was the end of that. A chance lost.

There was a nasty epilogue to this tale shortly after. First I learned that the YTS organisers who had refused to invest a couple of hundred pounds in my future had stumped up for another guy to be sent to Spain to learn how to become a professional golf caddy. More important, the girl I had been working with was forced to take a job at a swimming pool. I got a call one day to inform me that she had died at work.

My next YTS assignment was at a garage not far from my dad's work unit. It was a decent cycle ride there and back, and I thought I could make a go of it. I liked the idea of being surrounded by cars and motorbikes all day. It didn't work out quite like that. I don't know why the owner needed help to run the place, as there were more staff than customers on some days. He struggled to find me jobs to do at the best of times, but the final straw came when I arrived one morning and he asked me if I'd mind doing some gardening.

'No problem,' I said. 'What needs doing? I mowed the grass verge last week.'

'Ah, it's not the garage,' he replied. 'It's actually at my house. You may as well, there's fuck all to do around here today.'

It was then that I saw the real point of the YTS project – the government made it worthwhile for employers to take youths off their hands and, more important, off the unemployment statistics. But this guy was taking the piss.

I unchained my bike, cycled off and never returned.

On my way home I passed Dad's factory. He wasn't slow to get something for nothing and he'd had a couple of YTS kids on the books since the scheme started. But somehow he seemed to be managing to cock it up. While the garage guy seemed to be turning a profit from having me there, Dad moaned that he was paying too much to the scheme so they could, in turn, pay the kids.

I remember him moaning about the set-up one evening. There was a time when I would have drunk in his every word and agreed whole-heartedly without thinking. Not any more. Now I was more inclined to assume he'd done something wrong. It was just a feeling, but since my overdose everything he said or did seemed to warrant more scrutiny from me. He wasn't my hero any more.

In the end he pulled out of the YTS altogether and got a

new employee whom he could pay directly, without all the paperwork and, as he called it, the 'bullshit politics' of the scheme. It was a shortlist of one at the interview stage: me.

'You'll be seventeen soon enough,' he told me. 'Then you'll be really useful.' What he really needed was another driver. While I was still sixteen he started to teach me to operate the Bedford Midi van – properly this time, without me having to sit on his lap. Over the next few weeks, if there were journeys involving country roads, I'd be the one behind the wheel. As we approached a town, I'd pull over and we'd swap seats. It wasn't a bad life, but I couldn't wait till my birthday. 'As soon as I can drive I won't have to sit next to him,' I promised myself. 'I won't have to see him so much.' I couldn't wait.

Until I could drive, I had to put up with him. Some days were easier than others. I was still very immature. If he said something to make me laugh, I forgot my doubts about our past. If he was in a bad mood, I spent hours scheming how to inflict some sort of revenge on him.

'Revenge for what?' I asked myself.

It was a good question. Any answer I gave wouldn't stand up in a court of law. On some level I knew that all was not well between my father and me and it had something to do with the attack on me in the bathroom that had driven me to overdose on painkillers. I knew I was the one who had said 'no' to him. I knew I was the one who provoked his rage. But I'm sure he didn't have to be so rough. I'm sure that things just got out of control. Did he make a mistake?

It was no more than a 'feeling'. But sometimes a feeling is all a sixteen-year-old needs to act – and working with Dad every day meant I had the opportunity to make him pay.

Even though my alarm clock woke me up at 4.30 a.m. every

day, I'd still always be asleep again by the time he knocked loudly on my bedroom door a few minutes later.

'Duncan!' he'd hiss. 'Get your arse up.'

While I staggered around with my eyes shut for as long as possible trying to get dressed, Dad would go downstairs and make breakfast. After eating, I would make two flasks of coffee for our journey. One for me, one for him. If my father had known the special blend I used, I think he would have started making his own.

It was always the same thing that went through my head when I pissed into my father's flask, always anger and resentment. I still didn't fully appreciate what I had to be angry about – just that feeling – but that was enough to go on. I only squeezed a few drops of urine in each day, not enough for him to even taste, and it was probably destroyed by the boiling water added soon after. But it made me feel good. It made me feel I was doing something in some small way to get back at him for the hurt and confusion he had caused me, both physically and mentally.

Although my pranks were very childish, it took a lot of emotional effort to actually go through with them. A voice in the back of my mind was ever ready to say, 'He's still my dad.' By contrast, my father seemed to have the power to hurt me without trying. Despite my best efforts, I had always cared what he thought about me. I couldn't switch it off just like that. Obviously he didn't have the same restraint.

One incident sticks in my mind. Before I joined up with Dad full time, Andy had been a regular weekend helper. As part payment for his labours, my father bought him a Yamaha DT 125 motorbike. I was struck with jealousy. How dare he? He'd always refused to buy me one. 'Sometimes he barely even talks to me,' I thought, 'and he's buying my mate a motorbike. What the hell is going on?'

I thought of that every time I peed in his flask.

As it turned out, I didn't have to wait too long for my own wheels. Despite my erratic behaviour, thanks in equal measure to too much hash the night before and reservations about working with my father, he was impressed by my effort and when I said that my mates all had small 50cc motorbikes, he bought me one as well. The bikes weren't exactly Ducati Monsters – they only had a top speed of thirty mph – but they increased our daily travel range by more than 100 per cent. They also greatly improved our potential for fun. We were only sixteen, but the fact that we looked old enough to buy as much alcohol as we liked, and that we had fairly good access to some decent hash, meant that we could wreak havoc for miles around and still be back in time for dinner or bedtime.

Even with our new mobility, we still liked the sanctity of our various dens scattered around the area. Although Janice was tolerant of dope-smoking in her house, sometimes we needed a space of our own. Somewhere we wouldn't get hassled or harassed, whatever we got up to.

This wasn't such a problem when the weather was good. As long as it wasn't raining, there was always somewhere to go and hang out. We needed the dens for when it was miserable.

The best den we had was in a semi-derelict barn which was stuffed full of old wooden potato crates. Although it was in a fairly public location, and quite close to Andy's house, it was possible not to be seen going into the building if you approached from the riverbank side. So that's what we did. We arranged our den high up, near the roof, and moved all the crates around so you couldn't see it, or even the way up to it, unless you looked pretty hard. Considering we were occasional squatters, we were very house-proud. We decorated our little space and stole bits of carpet and mats to sit on. We had ashtrays and candles and at one time a small cassette player. All the creature comforts we needed, in fact.

The tape deck was our downfall. We were perfectly capable of being silent with just our spliffs for company, but throw in the chance of some music and all sense flies out the window. It wasn't exactly a rave in a field, but it was pretty close.

Somehow above the noise we heard a voice.

'Oi, you young buggers!'

'Shit,' I said. 'Who's that?'

The sound of four guys drunk on White Lightning and chilled on weed trying to be silent must be one of the funniest you'll ever hear. Unfortunately the farmer standing below us didn't think so.

'Get your ruddy backsides down here this instant!'

With our bikes and our booze and our tearaway lifestyle, we saw ourselves as easy riders. We were kings of the road. We were Marlon Brando in *The Wild One*. That was honestly how we saw ourselves.

The farmer had a different view. He saw us as four shit-scared kids trying not to cry.

His version was probably closer to the truth.

Gingerly we climbed down through the main hatch, and just when we were about to square up to the owner of the barn and take it like men, Jim yelled, 'Leg it!' and we shot out the door and across the field. Just to make sure there was no confusion between us and a gang of hard-nosed trouble-makers, Stephen yelled behind us, 'We are very sorry, sir.'

I don't know why he said it, but I know he regretted it instantly. From the moment we stopped to get out breath back, Andy was all over him, ripping the piss out of him and mimicking his voice. 'We're very sorry, sir, we're so sorry, sir, we're awfully sorry. Smack our bottoms, sir, we've been very naughty boys.' Stephen swore he said nothing of the sort, but it's funny how we all heard him say it.

Not only were we (at least one of us) very polite on exiting the barn, but I think the farmer must have been pleasantly surprised by the care we'd taken in looking after our little spot in the rafters. Other owners of isolated outbuildings weren't so lucky.

A few days later we broke into a warehouse in a nearby field, hoping to find booze or food. In the end we found everything but. The building was the head office of a catering company and while they had napkins, cutlery, plates and glasses, there was nothing to eat. Desperate to leave our mark on the place, Stephen suggested depositing something inside one of the dozens of accounts ledgers on the office shelves. The next thing we knew, he had pulled down his trousers and was squatting over the open book.

A few minutes later, the ledger was back on its shelf. As we left the building via the same hole in the roof by which we'd entered, we laughed at the thought of the catering staff trying to trace the source of the unpleasant smell.

The next few days were spent waiting anxiously for the local paper to be delivered each evening. What if we were seen? What if the owners told our parents that we'd shat on their property?

Shitting in public seemed to us, on some sort of primeval instinctive level, to be the worst thing we could do to rebel against the laws of our respective parents. There was no other reason for it. I don't know about Stephen's folks, but I could imagine even Andy's mum going berserk. And as for the apoplexy my parents would go into if they knew – that just made it all the more worth doing.

On another occasion we decided to vent our frustration on the whole village. We were bored as usual, it was a weekend and no one had any cash. We'd exhausted our narcotic options and decided there was nothing left to do but to go on a shoplifting spree around Billinghay. A plan was drawn up, starting at the post office, and taking in the convenience store, the newsagents and finally the co-op. The run took about thirty-five minutes and was the most exhilarating thing to happen to any of us that week. The adrenalin that surges through your body when you know you could feel a hand on your shoulder at any second is incredible.

When we had finished we went down to the riverbank to examine our booty. The inventory of stolen goods included:

1. Six tins of beer – Carling Black Label
2. Twelve bars (100 grams) of Cadbury's Dairy Milk
3. Twelve bars (25 grams) of Cadbury's Fruit and Nut
4. Nineteen Cadbury's Cream Eggs
5. Some Ritz cheese crackers
6. 112 assorted tampons, both Lilets and Tampax

To the untrained eye, the whole list is self-explanatory – except perhaps for the tampons. Why did we have them? The answer is simple: ammunition.

Any teenager who hasn't fired a wet tampon at a target is missing out. The recipe for mayhem is easy to follow: take one tampon – super plus are the weapon of choice. Unwrap it, dip it into a muddy river or puddle and remove when fully expanded. Baste tampon in either grit or soil and then prepare to serve. Grasp tampon by small piece of blue string, rotate throwing arm as fast as possible and fling at your mate or a passing motorist as hard as you can.

How many travellers along the A153 ever knew why they kept finding brown tampons stuck to the roof of their cars?

It was childish and it was anti-social on many levels. But pranks like this kept me out of the house physically. They also distracted me mentally. When I was wrapped up in such ridiculous high jinks I didn't have a care in the world. My mother's sharp tongue seemed a million miles away. My father, similarly, couldn't harm me out here. Not if I couldn't see him. Not if I couldn't even remember him for a few minutes.

At sixteen I thought I had all the mates I needed. Andy and Stephen, and to a lesser extent Jim, had always been there for me. They didn't know why I depended on them. I never let on that I regarded them as the family that I never had, that they were the one constant in my life. Perhaps they sensed it for themselves, because they never let me down, even when I didn't deserve it.

Dad hadn't demanded a flick for nearly two years, but I still couldn't get out of the habit of lying. I'd been doing it consistently for so long, I couldn't shake off the instinct. I used to play my mates off against each other just as I'd try to manipulate my father. It had become second nature for me to try to win some sort of emotional upper hand through sympathy or bravado, whenever the opportunity arose.

Sometimes I thought it would be more fun if it was just me and Stephen hanging out, or me and Andy over at his mum's place. I thought nothing of telling one mate that the other couldn't make it. It wasn't personal. I was looking after Number One.

I never really understood why I gradually became like that with my dad. Nobody taught me to behave in that way. Not overtly, anyway. What I do know is that as I grew up I realised he would do things for me if I did things for him in exchange. Sometimes I wanted to get a material return, like a new toy. On other occasions he would lie to protect me from Mum or the school, giving me freedom that other kids my age just didn't have. If I wanted to go somewhere, a quick word with him and it would happen. I didn't understand how it worked or why it worked, but I knew at some level that I could get my own way if I played it right.

I have no regrets about how I treated my father. It was probably a self-defence mechanism learned out of desperation. But I have no excuse for using the same mind-games and manipulation tactics on my mates. None at all.

I started to fully appreciate what I was doing wrong when I was introduced to a new circle of friends. Like so many of my best experiences as a teenager, I have Andy's family to thank for this.

Just being in the new crowd's company was like holding a mirror up to myself. Unfortunately, after so many years of duplicity, I didn't like the reflection staring back. Perhaps on some level I didn't mind lying to my usual gang – it's possible I associated them subconsciously with all the pain and sadness I had suffered in Billinghay. But the new guys who Andy introduced me to arrived with no such baggage. I felt different in their company, as though I had nothing to prove. Most important, I had nothing to hide.

A guy called Dave and his family moved in next door to Janice. He was closer to my parents' ages than mine, but quickly proved himself to be the coolest, nicest and most honourable bloke I'd ever met. If it was possible to adopt someone as a father, I would have petitioned for him immediately.

Through him I met a lot of other people, all of them as nice in their own way. One day Andy and I popped by to visit and there were three new faces having a kickabout in Dave's garden. No sooner had we been introduced to Susie, her boyfriend Tim and their pal Richard, than we all felt like firm friends. The three of them lived in Lincoln, a city about half an hour away. Richard told me he played for the Manchester United youth team and, from the way he dribbled and played 'keepy up' with a football, I believed him.

If anyone else had spun me a line like that in public and tricked me so openly, I would have been annoyed. But somehow it felt like harmless fun in this company. There was no malice. We were all friends having a laugh.

I was beginning to see how it was not through luck that the best people had the best mates. Neither of my parents had anyone they could honestly call a friend. I suspect they both put this down to circumstance. Dave taught me, among other things, that friendship has to be earned. You get back what you put in.

With Janice doing my father's bookkeeping, there was always the chance that he would pop round and ruin things with Dave and Co. I don't know what I imagined he would do, but

Dad had a knack for making himself the centre of attention. I would have been mortified if Dave or Richard had extended their friendship to him.

The more time I spent with my new friends, the more difficult I found it being in my father's company. Where they were open and warm, he was detached and controlling. He probably always was, but with every passing week I viewed him with a more critical eye. Increasingly I didn't like what I saw.

When Janice decided to give up helping Dad, he employed a part-time secretary to work at his office. The new employee was the daughter of his old colleague, John. The girl's brother, Robert, who I'd met a couple of years earlier, was also given work cleaning Dad's vehicles and generally helping out. Once I turned up to discover Dad teaching Robert how to ride a motorbike. The lad sat on the front of the saddle and my father reached round to drive the machine and they set off over the fields.

I didn't think too much of it at the time. My main emotion was relief. If Dad was distracted by someone else, I could do my jobs without having to spend much time with him. I also realised how much I would have hated to be the kid on the bike. For a moment I could picture yet again staring at the bathroom wall with my father's heavy breathing on my neck. I dismissed the image and got on with my chores as quickly as possible. The sooner I left the yard the better. It was becoming like an extension of home. Another place I wasn't comfortable going.

I was glad when Janice stopped working for Dad, because it meant I no longer had to worry about him sniffing around what I regarded as 'my territory'. It meant I could be my normal, natural self – something I could never be at home – and indulge in the things that made me happy with the people who were important to me. My first spliff with Dave was in Andy's house. It was there that I had my first trip on magic mushrooms as well. Janice calmly made Andy and me a cup of tea and even recommended a few records that we should play while taking them.

Janice was a forward-thinking parent. She didn't believe in driving her kids away by draconian laws that could never be followed. 'Do what I say not what I do' was not her way of thinking at all. She appreciated that we all have to grow up and experiment in things for ourselves. She knew full well we'd be trying out drugs somewhere, but she wanted us to do it where she could monitor the situation, give us a safe environment and keep an eye on us in case of problems. I thought she was really cool.

Dave never supplied me with any drugs. He was very careful about that. He never wanted to be in a situation where he could be accused of corrupting young people. On the contrary, I was often the one giving him hash. If I finished work early, I would scoot towards Lincoln and meet my new mate Tim half-way. Sometimes I'd light up with him, but usually I'd try to get back to the lads in Billinghay for a good session. Anything, as usual, rather than go straight home.

Of all my old friends, Stephen was the oldest, hitting seventeen before the rest of us. He had passed his test first time, and as a reward he was allowed to drive his mother's Talbot Horizon when she wasn't using it. One evening while I was getting ready to leave my dad's yard, he pulled up in the driveway. Jim and Andy were already in the car.

'Hop in, Dunc,' Andy called out. 'We've got places to go.'

I didn't have a clue what they were talking about, but they were providing a ready-made excuse not to go directly home. Obviously I leapt at the opportunity.

'Shove over,' I said to Jim, and I climbed into the back of the car.

I assumed we were going cruising as usual. We'd prob-ably find a place to pull over, then either stroll round to one of our dens scattered around the village or smoke some dope right there in the car – with the windows open, of course.

We drove to the village sports field and walked across to the play area by the youth centre. I was still none the wiser as to what they had in mind. I sat on one of the swings to light up, and expected the others to do the same. I was suddenly aware that they were just standing around, look-ing at me.

'What's going on?' I asked. 'You're giving me the fucking creeps.'

They looked at each other and then Jim said, 'Why do you bullshit us so much?'

'What are you on about?' I said, stunned.

'Don't be soft,' Stephen said. 'We're your mates. You treat us like we're pig shit. Where do you get off with all the lies and crap you come out with? What's your game? What are you up to? We're your fucking mates. Doesn't that mean nothing to you?'

I could see from their faces that they weren't messing around. My stories had caught up with me. I'd been playing them off against each other for so long to cover up what I was doing with Dad that I hadn't been able to stop even though it was over. I still told Andy one thing, Jim something else and Stephen another pack of lies if the mood took me. I couldn't help it. It was as if I was programmed.

'I only wanted to make them like me,' I reasoned to myself. All the cigarettes, the booze and the porn I had endless supplies of – they were all attempts to make me popular. They were also smokescreens to stop anyone from asking too many questions about my home life.

But somewhere I'd screwed up. Now they were asking questions all right. The biggest question, though, was, 'Am I going to tell them the truth?'

I decided yes. Yes I was. 'These are my closest friends. These are the only people on the planet I trust,' I thought. 'It's about time I was honest.'

And so I told them.

I didn't look at their faces. I just stared into the ground as I pushed myself back and forth on the swing, crying as I told them everything. From the first time that I remembered, to the first time my father had told me about. I told them about the Geoff Capes episode and the rape over the radiator. They still didn't know I'd tried to commit suicide that day. But now it would make sense. My 'mystery illness' that my mum told them about should become clear.

I talked for about five minutes non-stop. It might have been longer. Throughout I cried like a baby. I could see my tears dropping down and hitting the dry dirt under my feet.

As I spoke I felt the weight lift from my shoulders. 'Why didn't I do this years ago?' I thought.

Stephen came over and hugged me as I spoke, trying to soothe my tears. Jim started to pace agitatedly about, kicking the floor and slapping his forehead as if he was struggling to get the information into his brain.

Andy remained silent. He just stared at me, listening to my words. And then he snapped.

'I've had enough of this,' he yelled. 'It's all fucking lies, isn't it?'

'Easy, Andy,' Jim said, but Andy wouldn't be stopped.

'Don't you two see it's just another one of his lies? His old man wouldn't do anything like that. You know him as well as I do. He's too fucking nice.'

'I believe him,' Stephen said.

'Well, I don't,' Andy insisted. 'And how are we ever going to prove it, eh? He knows full well we're not going to march up to his old man and go, "Excuse me, Mr Fairhurst, are you a kiddy fiddler?" It's bullshit, I tell you. You don't want us to ask your old man that, do you, Duncan?'

'Ask him what you want,' I said with as much composure as I could muster. 'Tell him everything I've told you. See what he says.'

Andy shook his head anxiously. 'No, no, no,' he said. 'I've had enough of this crap,' and he walked away.

Stephen and Jim looked at me and at each other. Did they believe me or did they believe Andy? I could tell they weren't sure. Had I just made the biggest mistake of my life thinking I could trust them? What the fuck was going on? Andy was my best friend in the entire world. Look what the truth had done to him. Look how he had reacted. 'How can I ever tell another soul if this is what is going to happen?' I wondered.

And then another thought hit me. 'Is this it with me and Andy? Is this the end? My dad hasn't touched me for two years. I thought it was over. I thought I was free. Is that bastard going to mess up the rest of my life like he messed up the start?'

The answer, I feared, was yes. But only time would tell.

14

The Boy Who Cried Wolf

From the age of four until I was fourteen, I masturbated my father pretty much on demand. I never enjoyed giving him a 'flick', as he called it. My arm always ached soon after we started, and he would often get angry. I tried my best, I swear I did, but I found the whole procedure totally boring. I willed him to ejaculate, just so I could continue with my evening. Dinner, flick, *Top of the Pops*. Dinner, flick, playing with Lego. That kind of arrangement was a large part of my life for ten years.

Our relationship changed following my suicide attempt. His last physical contact with me was when he forced himself inside me. By taking those paracetamol tablets I put an end to that.

Would I have still acted as I did if I'd known the result? I honestly don't know. I had been conditioned for most of my life to equate giving Dad a flick with love. It was normal for me. That was how my father demonstrated that he cared.

When it stopped, at first I didn't notice. My two weeks in hospital had been a break. I assumed it would be business as usual when I was fully recovered. Hopefully not the violent stuff in my backside, but the normal 'loving'. I never enjoyed wanking him because it made me bored and tired. But if that's what kids do, who was I to argue?

It transpired that I never had to do anything like that to my father again. I'm grateful for that, but I wish he'd told me his plans. I wish he'd said to me, 'It's over. All that's behind us. You don't have to do that any more.' Then I could have relaxed. Then I wouldn't have spent years unable to take a shower without listening anxiously for the rattle of the bathroom door handle.

When I admitted my secret to my friends that night near Billinghay youth centre, I was just relaying the facts. Did I realise at the time that what my father had done repeatedly to me was wrong? No, I honestly don't think I did. I suspected but, for every hunch I had, I had a greater inner desire to be wrong. The consequences of being right were too intimidating to contemplate. Through a combination of cannabis and avoiding my father where I could, I kept those hunches out of my mind as much as possible.

I knew for certain that I didn't like it, but I didn't know it wasn't right. Even though Dad made it clear it wasn't a subject people talked about openly, I didn't know it was considered so bad. I knew I preferred to get drunk on White Lightning or high on hash than think about our bathroom sessions. I knew he had sworn me to secrecy, I knew he had alarmed me by saying he'd have to go to prison and be taken from the family if I told anyone. But I still did not know it was wrong. I did not know it was the thing the newspapers were calling paedophilia.

I did not know I had been abused.

I was in denial. At the very most, I was beginning to ask questions. Some of them were prompted by the silence from my friends on the subject of their dads' behaviour. Others came from seeing documentaries and magazine articles about a charity called Childline that was launched in 1986, when I was sixteen. A lot of what I learned about the people Childline was hoping to help reminded me of my own life. But again I thought, 'There must be a difference between me and them. My father loves me.'

I realise in hindsight that even a year after leaving school, and two years after my father's last physical attack on me, I still did not know what had happened to me. Not really. I did not even know what I thought about it. I was forced to believe so many lies, to live a lie for so long, and to block out my true emotions, that I honestly don't recall when the truth started to seep in. And when it did, I fought it. Even watching the Childline programmes, I fought it. And until I stopped fighting I would never be free.

Shortly after turning seventeen, I became 'useful', as my father put it. I think he was actually quite proud that I managed to pass my driving test first time, but he tried not to let that show too much. What he was really interested in was the fact that I could now drive my own van rather than just accompany him. Now we could get twice the business done.

As a treat for passing, Mum insisted they buy me a car of my own, a Mini. I was also allowed the full run of the van when I was not working. You could fit a lot of people in the back of that wagon. The Fairhurst Taxi Service – drop-outs and druggies our speciality – was in business.

For about a year I drove 300 miles a day, all over the UK, from Smithfield in London to Chesterfield to Leeds. I loved it. I was free.

If my parents thought that having gainful employment would set me on the straight and narrow, they were sadly mistaken. Cannabis was the only thing keeping me alive – that and a few other chemical aids. Every time the real world got a bit too close, one roll-up, one click of the lighter, one puff and I could escape.

I never took heroin, but anything else was fair game. Drugs had been the most important part of my life for a while already and I wasn't fussy.

I smoked a lot when I was driving. I was good. I could roll a three-skin joint, using hard Moroccan hash, motoring at 90 mph on the M1. Ninety-five per cent of my joints were perfect. The rest? Well they had a tendency to look like Hoover bags.

My average working day went something like this: arrive at Dad's warehouse about 5.30 a.m. Load my van in half an hour, and be on the road by 6. There were normally a few minutes when I was left alone while Dad hunted around for delivery instructions, and I always used them to roll the first joint of the day. A few minutes later I would pull out of the yard, throw a Doors tape into the cassette deck, and light up. Next stop oblivion!

The combination of the music and the Dutch (or Colombian) courage had a greated influence on my driving than the Highway Code did. By two o'clock I'd be back in the yard, deliveries done and tyres still burning. Dad would roll in a few hours later, having done an equal distance. If I had a death-wish, it was a productive one.

Once I'd mastered driving on weed, I felt I could handle anything. That wasn't quite true. The first time I tried the potent cannabis derivative called skunk I was alone in my van, just about to leave Billinghay. I remember starting to puff away as usual, but the rest is a blur. Before I got to the end of the road I'd thrown up all over my lap and nearly crashed the van and half a ton of chicken into a ditch. 'Fuck this,' I thought, and promptly reverted to the 'safer' option of skinning up.

The long hours with just my thoughts for company were tedious at first, but soon I was grateful. As well as putting some distance between me and reality, the regular cannabis consumption also helped me focus in a pain-free manner – almost as an observer of my own life – on what was happening to me. Unfortunately I did not like what I learned.

I was at the wheel of my father's Bedford van when I had my epiphany. 'I was abused,' I thought. 'I was raped. My dad's a paedophile.'

Part of me wanted to put my foot down and end my pain there and then, but instead I pulled over and tried to cry. No tears came out. I was too stunned. 'Why has it taken me so long to work it out?' I asked myself. 'It's been staring me in the face for years.'

I really had been in denial.

I realised that I had been kidding myself. When I'd confessed to my mates about why I lied so much, I'd blamed it on the stuff my dad did to me. But I didn't blame *him*. I never made the mental leap.

But the others had. That's why Andy had blown up like that. He knew exactly what I was saying. He knew I was accusing my old man of being a paedophile. And he didn't want to hear it. Like a lot of people, he wasn't comfortable admitting he even knew a child abuser in case it reflected badly on him. I've seen it in others. They don't initially think of anything other than how it affects them, how they might have been victimised in some way. 'I've shaken hands with a pervert – is there anything he did to me that I thought was suspicious at the time?' Compassion for the real victim comes later.

I cursed myself for my own naivety, but what was the point? Somewhere inside, I knew. I must have done. There was a reason that I hadn't once, in the two years since the overdose, even thought of asking my father for anything in exchange for a flick. It wasn't just because I didn't like it – that had never stopped me in the past. It was because I knew it was wrong.

I had known for a while. All the facts were there in my brain, in my memory. I'd gone over everything in my mind enough times. I just hadn't wanted to face up to what it meant. I hadn't been prepared to face the consequences.

I hadn't been prepared to recognise my own father as a child abuser.

I hadn't been prepared to begin a life without him in it.

I may have resisted the urge to crash the van into a tree that day, but I was soon doing the next best thing. 'I'm through with this life,' I promised myself. 'Wake me up when it's over.' Anything I could get my hands on to smoke, I would smoke. And I didn't care how I got hold of the money. What risk wasn't worth taking if it stopped me having to deal with my Dad and what he'd done? I'd thought it before, but now I knew why.

By declaring outright war on my father, at least in my mind, I was effectively condemning my mother to the same sentence. If the drugs I took to avoid dealing with Dad made me belligerent when I came home, she suffered as well. At the time I didn't consider her an innocent party. In fact I didn't consider her at all. I was so consumed by the need to block out my hatred for my dad through narcotics that very little else penetrated my consciousness.

I certainly never thought of confiding in her. In my logic, as Dad's wife she was somehow part of the problem. But even at my lowest ebb I knew that skinning up was only one answer. The alternative was to talk about my problems and get help.

'Fuck that,' I thought. 'Not after what happened last time.'

The looks on my mates' faces when I had told them the truth were still fresh in my eyes months later. And their words still hurt, especially those from Andy. Stephen did his best to understand and to make me appreciate how hard it was for them to comprehend what I was saying.

'We've heard it all before, Dunc,' he said quietly. 'You're the boy who cried wolf. You can't help yourself. You don't know when to stop.'

Getting high with my friends used to be fun, but now it was the best way to enjoy their company. We still had plenty of laughs and loads of naughty experiences together, but things were never the same. It was as though we hung out through habit not choice. The laughter didn't have the same innocence, and a lot of our once-friendly joshing was now delivered with an underlying edge. We all had our own issues and they impacted on how we got on with each other. We were all men with our own reasons to block out the world. While my mates knew mine, even if they didn't believe it, I was completely in the dark about everyone else's hang-ups. Even through the drug-induced harmony, you could feel the tension within the group.

Whereas once we only targeted our japes against a world we all felt didn't have a place for us, now we started to pick on each other. Andy was the most vicious, and for some reason I was always the butt of his humour. Once he said he had put some LSD in my beer and goaded me until I told him what hallucinations I could see.

'You fucking idiot,' he laughed, 'there's nothing in there. Bullshitter!'

I tried to laugh it off, as usual, but he seemed to be making another point apart from giving us all a giggle at my expense.

We still hung out as a pair, but less so, and never without some cannabis to mellow the mood. He started going down to London more and more to stay with his brother, who lived in a squat in Hackney, and I spent as much time as possible with Dave and Richard.

When I was eighteen Andy and his family moved from Billinghay to Leadenham, a place fifteen miles away. He was old enough to move out and fend for himself, so he could have stayed, but like me and the rest of our crowd he had yet to make the break. We all had driving licences and vehicles, so visits to and from each other's homes were still possible, but after a flurry at the start they began to get further apart until communication eventually dried up completely.

Like so many things, at the time I didn't really notice the relationship sliding. I was too busy with my new Lincoln buddies, and meanwhile the drugs I smoked to mask the emotions I felt about my father also hid the pain of losing Andy. But I do mourn the loss of friendship. We had some great adventures when we were young.

I'm sad about the way I let my father drive a wedge between

me and Andy. A few years later, however, he did something else far worse.

Out of the blue I had asked my father if he had heard from my old friend recently. The answer shocked me. 'Didn't I tell you?' he said. 'Andy died a while ago. Overdose. To be expected really.'

I was shocked. I'd heard rumours about Andy being a serious drug user in London, but I thought it was just gossip. Even though we hadn't been close for a while, I felt guilty that I didn't know before. 'What must Janice be going through?' I thought. First her husband, then her son. A few weeks later, however, I discovered through a friend that Andy was alive and well. My dad had lied.

I've thought about why he did it many times over the years. He just laughed when I confronted him. 'I was pulling your leg, you idiot.' But there must have been more to it than that. Had Andy repeated my accusations to him as he'd threatened to? Did Dad want to keep me away from Andy in case I talked to him about it some more?

I just don't know.

What I do know is that I should have broached the subject of my abuse with my father instead of letting it eat away at me inside, but I couldn't find the strength. He never mentioned it, obviously, and so I kept quiet too. But whereas Dad never seemed to give it another thought, judging by the way he was so 'normal' around me, I needed all the drugs I could afford, and many I couldn't, to block my feelings out. Perhaps I wasn't strong enought alone, but with my chemically en-hanced coping mechanism I could get by. And that, for the moment, was all I could hope for.

*   *   *

One of the good things about turning eighteen was coming into a bit of money. Mum had been putting a few pence away every week into one of her orange book insurance accounts that she had with the Pru, and it had finally matured. When she handed the policy over I noticed the date was wrong.

'It says 1986 on this, not 1988,' I said. 'There must be some mistake.'

Mum looked at me. 'There's no mistake,' she replied. 'I thought if you got your hands on this money at sixteen you'd throw it away. You're eighteen now. You're old enough to spend it wisely. If I were you I'd open another policy. That's what your sister's done with hers.'

'Yeah, maybe I will,' I muttered, thinking, 'or maybe I won't.' Three hundred pounds was a fortune to me. As if I was going to stick it all in the bank.

A few days later I arrived by ferry in the Hook of Holland, just as I had done with Andy and my father a few years earlier. But this time I was on my own. And this time I could do exactly what I wanted.

On the boat over from Harwich I met a guy with similar interests, which in a traveller to Amsterdam often means one of two things: prostitution or drugs. Without him I would have been blown away by the different smokes on offer, but he showed me the ropes and took me to the largest Bulldog coffee shop and gave me a quick introduction to getting high legally. We spent a few happy hours getting stoned together before going our separate ways.

A year or two later I saw him again. He was modelling jeans in one of my mother's Kays catalogues. Funny how things turn out.

In Amsterdam I found my spiritual home for a few days. I

didn't have a care in the world while I was there. I didn't even have any bad dreams or unpleasant trips. 'I don't think I've ever been so happy for so long,' I thought.

I didn't want the trip to end but I knew it had to. If I couldn't stay there, at least I could take some of the country back with me. And so I did – as much high-quality hash as I could afford. I certainly had enough friends to buy it from me when I got home, so it was a win-win situation – assuming, that is, that I didn't get caught by Customs.

With my old gang gradually fading into the distance back home, the time with Dave and his friends became more important. Every time I went round there were a few new faces, and they all took their host's lead and treated me like an adult. Dave was a wise old coot but he never patronised anyone, even if they were arguing from a position of bugger-all knowledge. He was patient, kind and interested in everyone's opinion. A really great guy.

I was eighteen when Dave decided he wanted to move back down south. As much as I didn't want him to go, I said I'd help him move. I borrowed a van from Dad and drove all his gear down to London. I wouldn't take any petrol money from him, so as a thank-you he bought me a ticket to the Glastonbury Festival.

That was one hardcore weekend. For a start most of Dave's mates were 'jumpers' – like thousands of others, their 'ticket' entitled them to hop over the dodgy perimeter fence when the security team weren't looking. Because Dave had a mobility problem, he walked in through the more traditional and more expensive entrance along with me and his son, Adrian.

I was blown away by the whole event. Even though as an eighteen-year-old I'd tried my fair share of LSD, speed and other hard drugs, I was almost too intimidated to leave my tent. Everywhere I looked there were deals going down, right there in the open. 'Wicked, isn't it?' Dave said. And he was right.

A supply of good ganja and a demijohn of scrumpy were all I needed to have a great time, and I had both right on my doorstep. 'I'm definitely coming back next year,' I thought.

The drugs legislation in the Kingdom of Glastonbury might be relaxed to the point of non-existence, but outside its borders things are a bit different. The steady flow of stoners, and worse, coming out of the field must have kept the local coppers' arrest rates up for the whole year. As I drove out, I noticed they were doing random road stops on all the routes out of the site. It must have been like shooting fish in a barrel. Surprise, surprise, I think they got lucky with everyone they stopped.

They certainly did with me.

I was found to be in possession of four tabs of LSD, a small amount of cannabis and some magic mushrooms. What were the odds of that? I was pretty pissed off. 'We're just trying to have some fun,' I said. 'You must have some proper criminals to go after?'

'Possession of drugs makes you a proper criminal,' one policeman pointed out. 'So button it.'

I was charged and released on bail to appear before Tisbury and Mere magistrates later in the year.

'Shit,' I thought. 'How am I going to keep this from Mum?'

By the time I got home that night, I discovered the short answer: 'I'm not.'

To give Mum credit, she played it cool for a while. I told her I'd been stopped for speeding on the way home. 'So don't be surprised if I get a court summons in the post,' I warned her.

'For speeding, you say?' she asked.

And then World War III broke loose.

According to her, the Lincolnshire police had been round 'in their hundreds', turning the house upside down in their attempts to find evidence to bring down the notorious criminal D. Fairhurst. 'Do you know how stupid I felt when I opened the door?' she screamed. 'I thought you'd been in an accident. I wish you had!'

The ultimate shame was when two coppers went through my sister's underwear drawer. 'Lord knows what they were hoping to find in there!' Mum said. 'Poor Jo. How do you think that makes her feel? Do you have any idea what you've done? You should be ashamed of yourself. I'm ashamed of you. You're nothing but trouble.'

Mum's tirade worked. It was the kick up the backside I needed.

Two days later I moved out of the family home. 'Now I can play by my rules,' I thought. 'And there's nobody who can stop me.'

15

The Second Half Belongs to Me

I was nineteen when I became a drug dealer.

Then I liked to think it was the making of me. The day I became a man, a 'player'. Looking back, it was another step down a road I didn't want to go down. It was another inch closer to a place I wouldn't want my worst enemy to visit.

At the time, I had no choice. I was doing my best to cope with what I had.

Some people hide with their head in the sand. I hid my head in a cloud. A cloud of marijuana. And the rest.

For £850 I purchased ten ounces of blond Lebanese cannabis. I say 'purchased' but it was strictly an 'on credit' deal. I had never seen an amount of money like that in my life. Even Dad didn't leave that much cash lying around.

Blond Lebanese was unusual at the time, and I banked on this attracting me a decent return. Getting in debt to a dealer to the tune of almost a grand without a means to pay it back is as good as signing a suicide note. I had to make it work.

At the time, 'soap bar' or 'sticky black' were the common types. The gear I had wasn't the strongest, but it had novelty value. Selling an eighth of an ounce at fifteen pounds a pop meant I recouped an impressive £1,200. I would have been in line for another £200 if I hadn't taken it on credit, but even £350 for a few hours' work was not to be sneezed at. On top of that I had my own cheap supply of cannabis and more friends than I could shake a stick at.

Everyone is nice to you if you have a lot of drugs.

I also increased my own experimentation at this time. I never took heroin, but anything else was fair game. Drugs had been an important part of my life since I was a kid. They'd helped me stay alive. Now they were starting to earn me a living when I had no other options.

Over the next few months I had near-death and over-whelming religious experiences on LSD. I had forty-minute whole-body orgasms on ecstasy and I encountered plenty of things I'd never even heard of. The most powerful drug I took by choice was a little-known psychedelic called 5-Methoxy-N, N-Dimethyltryptamine. I might not have been so keen if I'd known it was the synthesised form of pus from a cane toad's eye socket gland.

I only ever came across a few hardcore junkies, and most of them hid it quite well. One couple I know in London work in television. They chase the dragon all the time and think nothing of going into work smacked up.

Others are too far gone to care about such things as jobs. A junkie I met in Bristol had to do press-ups before he could find a place to inject.

Dave, Janice and the other wise old heads who educated me in drugs all looked down on shooting up. 'Stay away from opiates,' they preached. Of the friends I knew who didn't follow this advice, many are no longer with us.

*   *   *

Two of my newer friends, Susie and Tim, were as important in my life as Dave and Janice. When I decided to move out of my parents' house, they were the people I turned to. Actually they turned to me. They must have discussed it already, because they brought up the idea of me moving in with them in Newport, Lincoln. They even drove me down to my court hearing in Tisbury. The way they looked at it was simple. 'A friend of Dave's is a friend of ours . . .'

Dave still popped up every so often from London, and if I had to work, he would come along for the ride. Even though I'd moved out of home, I still did jobs for my father. In a strange way we actually got on better now that we weren't together all the time. Once he asked me to clean out a large chest freezer that had broken. I didn't mind the work. The problem was, it had been full of frozen chickens when it malfunctioned. Now it was full of chickens that had defrosted to the point of rotting.

I have never smelled anything quite so vile in my life. Just thinking about it now makes me struggle not to retch.

This particular task coincided with one of Dave's visits, and he generously offered to help out. Unfortunately his stomach is even weaker than mine. The stench of one green, decaying bird was enough to have him bent over, coughing, in the yard. There was no way he would be any use fishing out the remaining three hundred.

The only way to eliminate the putrid aroma was by burning them. While I fought the urge to vomit with every trip to the freezer, Dave got half a dozen wooden pallets together and started an impressive bonfire. Guy Fawkes night came early to Billinghay that year.

Dave was just getting some colour back into his cheeks when Richard and two other mates, Steve H. and Tom, turned up at the warehouse. They'd heard that Dave was in town and tried to persuade us to go out with them.

'I've got a better idea,' I said. 'It's a shame to waste the biggest barbecue this village has ever seen.' I ran back into the warehouse and came out with three perfectly healthy frozen chickens. 'Anyone hungry?'

It was the start of a long night. All of us happened to have a bit of pot tucked away, and Steve was even able to produce an impressive Rastafarian clay pipe called a 'chillum'. We had to huddle together to stop the wind blowing out the pipe's flame, but, a few rounds later, we were all high as kites. On the third round, the chillum was passed to Dave. Even though he was the most experienced among us, something went down the wrong way and instead of toking he gave an almighty cough into the pipe. It was so powerful that the chillum exploded in his face, sending a shower of red-hot hashish pieces into the air. There was no escape. We were all covered. The ashes went in our hair, down our necks and burned through every piece of clothing they touched.

It was pretty funny at the time. I can only imagine how ridiculous it looked to anyone wandering by. The sight of five stoners leaping around like epileptics doing a rain dance as we tried to put our clothes out must have been hysterical.

Apart from when I was helping Dad, the only other times I went home were to get a decent meal inside me and to rob money. That was what it had come to. Take, take, take.

'Do I care?' I asked myself. 'Pass me another spliff and I'll think about it.'

Money was a problem. In the early days my drug deals were few and far between. Like most people, I only sold to friends. I wasn't brave enough to seek out new punters. Not yet.

I couldn't claim housing benefit because I had left home voluntarily, so work was a priority – any work. I got a job in Newport cleaning windows. Next I worked in a garage and then for a chain of hotels. It was all depressing, demeaning work. But I didn't mind. I arrived stoned, got drunk at lunchtime and drifted through the afternoon in my own world until it was time to go home for some serious smoking.

Even through the permanent haze, for the first time in my life I felt like I belonged, like I was at the centre of something. Like I mattered to other people. In Billinghay, everything depended on Andy's approval. He was the one with the cool mum and the cool house. He provided the weed and the place to get stoned. He was the one offering the rest of us refuge from our shitty family lives. If he and I had fallen out seriously then I personally would have had nowhere to hang out and our little group would have fizzled out.

Which is exactly what happened when he moved out of the village.

In Lincoln I was independent. I was accepted for being me and no other reason. Once Andy moved to London, even Jim and Stephen swung by as well. My home, with Tim and Susie, was the new place to get stoned. It was a big house, with a garden, and dozens of pot-heads could while away the evenings without feeling cramped.

There were a couple of alternative haunts nearby. A bunch of good guys hung out in Clairmont Street. Some of my friends got me into that circle, but I always felt like an outsider. It was the same story at a famous squat in the heart of the town. I went there a few times with Rich, but they made it obvious I wasn't cool enough to fit in. No one was unpleasant, it was just clear that I only had a 'visitor's permit'.

It was a hardcore den of iniquity then, which was shorthand for a place where everything you wanted could be found. These days it's more likely to host swingers' parties than tripping sessions. I'm glad I got out when I did.

In spite of my early initiation into mutual masturbation, porn and orgasms, talking about sex was not something that came to me naturally. It still isn't. For so many years I was oblivious to the fact that what I was doing was even remotely related to sex. Sex happened between men and women. That is what I was taught by the man who was abusing me. I guess he thought that if I didn't think it was sex, I was less likely to drop him in it with a careless remark.

My fascination with the bodies of young girls, including my sister and my school friends, seems extreme to me now. All kids play 'doctors and nurses', but I think I indulged more than was healthy. My early exposure to hardcore pornography desensitised to a large extent any instincts I might have had about sexuality. Women were objects. One acquired these objects through negotiation. Possibly even force – that's what happened to me. At no point did emotions enter the equation.

Knowing that my mother was beaten by my father on several occasions reinforced this view. That was another reason I was relieved to get out of their house. All around me I saw perfectly healthy relationships being played out between equals. Tim and Susie were a good example, but there were dozens of others. Like so much of what I'd been raised to think of as normal, I knew my instincts on women were out of kilter with the real world. Knowing it was only the first step, though. Actually fighting the hang-ups enough to have a proper relationship with a woman still seemed out of my reach.

Living in Newport and being part of a large circle of friends, most of them off their face on something or other, meant that I had more opportunities with girls than at any time in my life. Weed does that to you. It makes you love everyone.

It also takes away any semblance of a sex drive.

I would spend hours cuddling a girl in my lounge, or flirting with her, thanks to the aphrodisiac of cannabis. No one has any personal borders in a scenario like that. We'd all share our most private thoughts during those sessions. Sharing our bodies was a natural progression.

We might kiss, we might slide our hands under each other's clothes. But anything further was just a physical impossibility. There was no way I could get close to an erection, not spaced out on weed.

At clubs it was the same story. I was either ripped on speed or blind drunk. Most girls wouldn't touch me with a barge-pole, and the ones who would soon lost interest. Even during conversations with strangers in bars the only thing on my mind was planning my next trip or looking out for a dealer to score a few pills. The choice between going to bed with a woman or embarking on my next three-day speed binge was a no-brainer.

That was my life. Those were my priorities. That was the value system I'd left home with.

Only one person in the world had ever given me an orgasm. My father. As much as I wanted to experience the touch of a woman, it was too hard to blot out my past. 'What if I think of him while she's touching me?' I thought. 'What if I can only get it up with him? What if I can never have sex with a woman?'

I couldn't bear to find out. Not sober, anyway. But the amount of drugs I needed to get over the fear meant I'd never be able to perform anyway. I was barely conscious half the time.

All that changed when I met Rachel.

Not for the last time in my life I have Rich to thank for this turn-up. He'd seen me struggle to get over my mental hurdles with women. Without knowing the truth, he put it down to shyness. 'We're going to have to get you sorted out,' he told me.

One night, after the local pubs closed, we went to a heavy metal club called Lasers. I quite liked the music, although I wasn't really into the goth scene like most of the customers there. The main reason for me going was to keep the alcohol flowing and to have another spliff. The main reason for Rich going, I discovered, was a little different.

We'd only been in there a few minutes when he walked over to a pretty girl clad head to toe in black and said, 'Hi, what's your name?'

Cool as you like, the girl replied, 'Rachel.'

'Hi, Rachel, my name's Rich and this is my good friend Duncan.' He pointed to me as if I was Exhibit A. 'Why don't you two get to know each other while I go to the bar?'

He gave me a slight nudge in the back as he walked past, and that was that. When Rich returned a few minutes later we were snogging for Britain.

I don't know why this time was different, but it was. Maybe it was the fact that my friend had taken an interest in my situation, so I wasn't on my own as usual. Even without knowing the truth, Richard cared enough about me to sense something was wrong. The very idea of him trying to put it right in his own way was enough to wake me up from my sexual stupor.

I realised I had been waiting to fall in love all my life. I'd been hiding the truth for too long, buying it under the empty Tennants cans and Rizla wrappers that fuelled and protected me.

What I didn't know that night in Lasers was that Rachel was only fifteen. I was nearly five years her senior, and it felt incredibly naughty when I found out. But she was mature for her age, and it wasn't as if I was a Casanova with a string of loved-and-left women in my wake.

Rachel and I went out for several months. I had finally found someone to be close to. It wasn't about sex, although I hoped that would come. My priorities were old-fashioned and romantic. I wanted to walk in the park holding hands, to get notes and letters from someone who cared about me. I wanted the things I'd never seen my parents have. I didn't want to hide behind the drugs any more. Not with her.

The less I depended on the speed and booze for my mental well-being, the more at ease I acted. As I gradually let more and more of my real personality through my narcotic defence mechanisms, Rachel began to see there was something beneath the surface, something I wasn't telling her. 'I can't believe this girl's only fifteen,' I thought. 'She knows me better than any adult I've ever met.'

Because she was so mature and because I respected her so much, I started contemplating the idea of telling her the truth. It wasn't an easy decision. 'Christ, she's just a kid, and I've only known her a few months,' one part of my brain was yelling. 'The last three people I told called me a liar. What the fuck's she going to do?'

But Rachel was different from Andy, Stephen and Jim. I'd only known her a fraction of the time I knew them, but we had connected on a higher level. She was my soul-mate. 'I'm not going to lie to her like all the others,' I promised myself. 'She deserves honesty.' And so the decision was made. I just had to pick my moment.

'I know there is something,' she whispered to me one day as we lay on my bed. 'Why don't you tell me what it is? Tell me what's bothering you.'

Seeing the look of genuine concern on her face, I could have cried there and then.

So I told her.

When I confessed to Andy, Stephen and Jim, I was still in the dark myself about what had really happened to me. I told them that my dad had masturbated me and that I'd masturbated him. I told them I didn't like it and I knew it wasn't as normal as he made out. But at sixteen I didn't know it was wrong. I didn't know it was illegal. I didn't realise I was a victim of sexual abuse.

I didn't know my own father was a paedophile.

But now I did, and I told Rachel all of it. I didn't pull any punches. I had nothing planned and I sobbed like a baby throughout. Even though she had never seen a grown man cry before, Rachel nursed my head in her arms and kissed my hair. 'Keep going,' she said, when I looked like drying up. 'I'm listening.'

She was just as comforting afterwards. We stared at each other in silence for a while, and then she told me she cared for me and was proud that I'd been able to share it with her. It couldn't have gone better from my point of view, apart from one thing. I'd chosen to unburden my soul on a school night, which meant there was a curfew to be observed back at Rachel's house. We kissed before she left and I promised to call the next day.

A few hours later, with a weight lifted from my shoulders, I shared a spliff with Rich and told him the same story. 'I'm on a roll,' I thought. 'If a teenager can cope with my story, my mate can.'

I was right. If Richard had been a friend before that point, he somehow went up a few notches thereafter. There were no tears this time, but he made it very clear that my years of suffering in secret were over. 'You're not alone any more, Duncan,' he told me. And for the first time in my life I think I believed it.

We briefly discussed some options open to me. 'You can get your old man put away, you know,' Richard explained. 'I'll back you up. You won't be on your own.'

It hadn't occurred to me before. I was just happy to get by from day to day. I was just happy to survive what my father had done to me. Pissing in his flask, robbing a few quid – that was the level of revenge I'd come up with. Getting him put in prison was a new one on me. But could I do it? Could I go through with it?

'With the right support, yes, I think I can,' I thought. 'With Rachel and Richard, I think I can do it.'

With a spring in my step, the next day I decided to go down to the school to collect Rachel after class. I guess I must have looked a bit weird hanging around the gates – too old to be a student, too young to be a parent, too scruffy to be up to any good. But I didn't care. I couldn't wait to see her again, to thank her for understanding everything.

I didn't get the chance that night. Rachel didn't come out

the gates as usual. When I called at her house, her mother told me she was staying at a friend's. I telephoned the next day and the next, each time with the same result. 'I'm sorry, Duncan, she's not here. I'll tell her you rang.'

'What the hell's going on?' I thought. But inside I knew. What had I been thinking? She was fifteen. What was I doing telling her all that shit about child abuse? 'You've screwed up again,' I told myself. 'You've screwed up royally this time.'

And once again, it was my father's fault.

'He'll pay for this,' I promised myself. But no sooner had the thought entered my head than it disappeared. 'Who am I kidding? If my girlfriend can't handle it, if my three best friends call me a liar, what chance have I got of convincing a jury that I've been abused?'

It was a blow I hadn't expected to be dealing with that day. 'I've got no chance. No chance at all. I'm back at square one. No girlfriend, nothing to live for. The bastard's won again.'

The only good news was I'd been there before. I had a ready-made escape plan to get me out of the real world at a moment's notice. In case of emergency, swallow this. 'Drugs and drink have got me this far,' I thought. 'Onwards and upwards.'

After a couple of pretty clean months with Rachel, I threw myself back into my old ways. The world could piss all over me and I wouldn't care. I probably wouldn't even notice.

A few weeks later, Tim and Susie split up, which in effect made me homeless. I wish I'd been sober enough to care more. I really like Susie. She is one of the good guys. I learned that the same can't really be said of her ex-boyfriend.

Drugs are addictive. Everyone knows that. I've known a lot of users and a lot of dealers. The only ones worth the time of day are those who put their friends before their habit. It's not easy. I speak from experience. But when you depend on your mates as much as I've had to, you must get your priorities right. Tim, unfortunately, let his addiction wreck things for him.

It all came to a head one day when I got a new batch of cannabis to sell. It was good stuff: ten ounces of Slate Moroccan. I had a few buyers lined up, but for now I stashed it under my bed and went out. The next day I went to get an ounce to split and sell. There were only nine left.

If Tim had come up to me and said, 'I'm sorry, mate, I was a bit short – I owe you for that', we would have been cool. He was like a brother to me. I would have given the lot to him if he'd asked. But he didn't.

'I haven't touched your fucking stash,' he told me. 'I swear to you. I haven't been near it.'

I knew him well enough to know he was lying. He must have had money troubles that he didn't want to share with me. I guess the split with Susie was playing on his mind. Maybe that was going to cost him a few quid which he didn't have. But in my book that's when you want your mates around you. You don't start to rob them and lie in their faces when you need them most.

I should know. I'd been down that road. I'd treated my mates like idiots. I could tell when it was being done to me.

What made it worse was the fact that Tim knew I'd got the stuff on tick. If I didn't sell it, I couldn't pay my supplier. If there is one thing I've learned in life, it's that you always pay your dealer. Always.

By stealing from me, Tim was knowingly pushing me a step closer to a smack in the face, just for starters, from a couple of heavies. You don't do that to your mates.

The day I moved out, I took all Tim's CDs and sold them at a secondhand shop. 'That should cover his ounce,' I thought. It was petty, and I hated myself for doing it, but I had a debt to pay, and after the way he'd treated me, there was no option. 'I'm not taking a going over for that creep.'

Living on my own not only meant I missed the company of Susie and, in a sad way, Tim, but also increased my overheads. My shoplifting skills had been honed in Billinghay for fun, but now I needed them to survive.

Stealing to eat is easy when you don't know the victims. As long as I made sure my targets were faceless corporations, who's to care? Not me, not in the state I was in. Life becomes very simple when you're hungry. You go to a supermarket, get a trolley and put some things in it. Then you get a pork pie and eat it while wandering round the store. Then maybe a scotch egg, a few sandwiches, a bit of cake, a couple of cans. 'You've got to try before you buy,' I thought. Except I had no intention of buying. After my lovely meal I'd leave the half-full trolley in an aisle near the door and stroll out.

There are enough supermarkets in Lincoln to have three square meals a day without being caught. Putting clothes on your back takes a bit more preparation.

To get anything decent out of a fashion store you really need one of their bags. The good news is that to get one all you have to do is saunter in with any old broken carrier and say, 'Any chance of one of your bags? Mine is knackered.' Now you're equipped to return at a later date.

Shortly after the store opens seems to be a lucrative time. Most of the staff are still yawning through their first coffee. In-store security is thinking about the sports pages. A typical hit saw me walk in at nine o'clock with my pre-acquired bag. I went straight to a pair of Nike trainers I'd already spotted and put them in the bag. Then I picked up two pairs of Levi's and took them to the changing room. I snipped the tags off one pair and put them in the bag as well. Then I walked out, handed the other pair over to the assistant and said, 'Not really my style,' and strolled out. The security guy saw my bag and was none the wiser.

Sometimes it pays to look over your shoulder. I liked to hover outside the store for a few minutes, because then you don't look like an obvious thief. 'Sorry, I completely forgot I hadn't paid – if I was on the rob, I would have been half-way to Peterborough by now,' was my stand-by excuse. On this occasion I sat on a bench directly outside the shop and watched life go on as normal inside. I smoked a cigarette, then walked off to see my mate Daz who lived on a canal boat on the River Brayford. 'Life is good,' I thought. At the time, I think I believed it.

Being able to shoplift is like an insurance policy. If you have no money, you can always eat.

Living hand-to-mouth you only really think about the next meal, the next place to sleep, the next pill to pop or joint to roll.

Most of the crimes I committed were what I called 'victimless'. They were drug deals where I was feeding desire, or where I siphoned off a few quid from organisations that would never suffer, even if they noticed. If individuals were involved, they were usually dealers who deserved it.

In my drug-fuelled rationalisation I justified my crimes on the basis that 'normal' people weren't being affected. But that was not always the case. Occasionally I stole from innocents. I can't condone the behaviour now, but I was at my lowest ebb.

In Billinghay the worst thing I did was to burgle a sweet old pensioner. It was the brainwave of her grandson, and I went along with it. He knew where she stashed her savings and her booze. He also knew she liked a kip in the afternoon. In those days I had cigarettes to pay for.

When it comes to drugs, you get even more desperate. I took my opportunity when I went into a small corner shop in Newport. The doorbell jangled as I went in, but no one came out from the back. I walked around the store, picked up a few bits and bobs and put them down on the counter. Still no one appeared. I called out; nothing. I leaned across, opened the till and grabbed all the tenners. I knew it wasn't right, and I hesitated. But when I left I had 120 quid in my pocket. The old biddy who owned the shop lost a week's profit, but it would keep the dealers from my door for another day or two.

Events like that were not unusual.

It's amazing how time drifts by when you're high. Day blurs into day. Week into week. Month into month. Before I knew it, I was twenty years and 365 days old. Somehow I'd reached twenty-one. There were times when I had thought I wouldn't see tomorrow. There were times when I had prayed I wouldn't wake up the next day. Now I was 'coming of age'.

If my family hoped that impending maturity would be a wake-up call for me, they were disappointed. If I was going to get 'the key to the door', I wanted to be off my face. 'Let's party!' I told Rich.

It was certainly a memorable night.

It started with two lines of pink champagne – very strong amphetamines – shared with a pal called Long-haired Fred, then we were off to the Jolly Brewer public house. In a more sober moment I would have been touched to be joined by so many friends. But there was no way I could be sober because each guest bought me a drink. Spirit, lager, spirit, lager – there was so much alcohol heading my way that at some point I decided that I needed to look for Rachel.

The idea of being lonely with so many friends around me that night was laughable. But I was. I hadn't thought about Rachel for months, but I did now. I had opened my soul to her. Somewhere in my drunken, tripping brain, I seemed to be aware that my life of pills, roll-ups and alcohol wasn't what I needed in the long term. If only I could have admitted that when I was sober.

Not surprisingly, I didn't find Rachel that night. But somebody found me.

I woke up at three in the morning in a police cell. From the noise outside, I could hear all hell breaking loose in the corridor.

'What have I done? What have they got me for?' I was worried. Even though I had a banging headache, I knew I hadn't managed to get through all the LSD I was carrying at the start of the evening. 'I'm busted now.'

I rang the bell for some attention. Nothing. I rang again. And again. Eventually a policeman's face appeared at the hatch in the door and he asked what my problem was.

'Can I have a glass of water, please?'

'Forget it.'

He slammed the hatch shut, and that was the last I saw of him.

I had a look around the cell. It was bare, with no mod cons: no toilet seat, no chair, no mattress.

For three hours I feared the worst. I knew it was only a matter of time before I was handed a massive drugs charge.

And since it wasn't my first offence, this time I'd be looking at more than a slap on the wrist. I was carrying enough gear to fuel the five thousand at the start of the evening. I genuinely couldn't remember the last few hours. (So much for my memorable night.) Who knows what I had been holding when I was picked up. At the very least, I knew they were going to find the strips of 'strawberry' acid I was carrying in a matchbox.

At six in the morning the door opened and I was dragged out to be 'processed'. 'This is it,' I decided. 'I'm going down.'

Still buzzing from a vast quantity of speed, but with the onslaught of a giant booze hangover just kicking in, I was a bit of a mess as I stood before the desk sergeant.

'Hold out your hand,' he said.

I did as I was told.

Thwack!

He hit my palm with a plastic ruler. Jesus, it hurt!

'Other side,' he said. I dutifully turned my hands over.

Thwack! The same thing again to my knuckles.

'Now, I'm going to charge you with being drunk and disorderly and resisting arrest,' he said.

'I wonder how strongly I resisted?' I thought.

'Bottom line: I'll let you go now but I don't want to see you here again,' the sergeant said. 'I've had a look through your wallet and I can see you were celebrating. Now piss off and behave.'

I started to leave the room when he called me back.

'Oh, Mr Fairhurst, one more thing,' he said.

'What now?' I wondered.

'Happy birthday.'

I couldn't remember the last time a stranger had been so

randomly thoughtful towards me. It felt nice. I think he actually smiled as he threw a clear plastic bag over to me. Inside were my shoes, belt and wallet, plus several other items which I had to sign for. A pack of Regal King Size (thirteen in the box), sixteen pounds in cash, two sets of keys, 33 pence in change – and one box of matches.

Leaving the station was more nerve-wracking than walking out of Marks & Spencer with two bags stuffed full of unpaid-for designer clothes. I fully expected a hand on my shoulder at any moment. 'It must be a wind-up,' I thought.

But no. I got all the way home before I dared to look in my matchbox. Inside were the two LSD strips I'd been storing. I always wrapped in tens, and all twenty were present and correct. And the police had missed them! Happy birthday to me indeed!

If I'd lost that stash I would have found more. That was my main source of income at the time. And what's more, everyone around me knew it. Word was spreading about me on the street. Complete strangers knew they could get what they wanted from Duncan Fairhurst.

When I was twenty-two and living on the aptly named Scorer Street in Lincoln, I fell ill with appendicitis, then peritonitis. For the third time in my memory I was rushed into hospital for an emergency operation.

While the surgeons worked their magic, somebody decided it was a good time to burgle my flat.

It wasn't the best news to be met with when the ambulance took me home. I made a few enquiries and learned that the culprit was a smackhead who, knowing I was a dealer, felt he could lay his hands on some cash and some gear if he broke in. Anything that was portable had disappeared, from my 250 vinyl albums to my hundreds of CDs and my beautiful Technics hi-fi.

Word had it my £700 hi-fi was sold for fifty quid.

I never got my belongings back, but the thief was hospitalised for his trouble. News of his naughtiness got out and he was tracked down and beaten severely. At no point did I give the order to hurt him. But the people I supplied were pissed off, and so were the people who supplied me. There was nothing I could do, with eight stitches in my stomach. But I didn't have to. Even though I had nothing to do with the punishment, I confess I lit a cigarette to celebrate when news reached me.

I was at a low personal ebb. I had never imagined a day when I would take pleasure in violence. What was happening to me? I never used to be like this. But that was before I realised my father had treated me like his personal sexual servant. Had I picked up from him the idea that some people don't have any human rights? Was his vile mind polluting my own mind? Even through the wall of drugs I had been so studiously erecting?

My fame as a player seemed to be growing day by day. I feel sorry for everyone who suffered as a result. I promise I never originated anything, although I rarely stepped in to prevent violence in my name. Something else I know from experience is that being punched hurts. If I can avoid it, I will.

Once a rival dealer took it upon himself to get me a reputation as a psychopath. 'If people think you're nuts you won't get any grief,' he assured me. Like a naïve fool I believed him. In reality he was warning people not to deal with me when they could deal with him.

Occasionally I did something which reinforced my 'psycho' image. Once, at a rave, a dealer told me he had slept with a girl

I fancied. Something possessed me and I remember head-butting a wall a number of times. Crowds gathered to watch. I barely broke the skin on my forehead, but the blood spread a lot. 'Don't mess with him,' was the message. 'He's a nutter.'

Afterwards I sat down with my love rival. 'The girl is mine,' I said.

'You've got it,' he replied. 'No hard feelings.'

Other events were less intentional but equally effective.

Once I was walking back from a kebab shop with a customer when someone grabbed my shoulder from behind. Without thinking I swung my elbow round to shake the hand off, and accidentally connected with the side of the guy's head. He went down like a stone. I stood over him and realised I had no idea who he was or why he had touched me. I was terrified I'd hurt him for no reason.

But my companion didn't know that.

'That was fucking awesome,' he said, then ran off.

Even though that incident was unplanned, I let stunts like that work to my advantage. I could get into clubs without being checked by bouncers, which meant I was able to smuggle drugs in effortlessly.

Working the late-night venues was not my preferred way of doing business, however. I went to clubs to dance and try to get laid, not to worry about deals and whether I accidentally dropped a fifty-quid note when I put my hand in my pocket. On an average night out I would take some blow, a pill or two and a quarter of speed and enjoy myself. The night-times were about me.

Even though I was making a living from selling, I was still a user. Most of my transactions took place in public arenas, but I preferred a bit of privacy when I used the goods myself. One of my favourite haunts was at the top of Lincoln Cathedral. It took half an hour to climb the surrounding scaffolding (during the day workmen were repairing the roof) but the view and the silence made it more than worthwhile.

For the time I was up there, I was thirteen again, hanging out in a den with Andy and the gang, hiding from the world.

At times like that, or when sitting beside a river, I realised that drugs were not about parties. They were not necessarily about fitting in. You can learn a lot about yourself using them in the right setting.

I was pleased to discover that I wasn't the only one benefiting from a little self-reflection. One stoned weekend I was with Richard in the Arboretum Park. It was late summer and we were experiencing the unique effects of a few magic mushrooms at the same time as attempting to juggle. I don't know what Richard was seeing, but there was no way I could differentiate between the real and the imaginary balls in the air.

When Rachel walked between us I assumed it was another hallucination. But I was wrong. I hadn't seen her for two years and here she was. Still a goth, I noted, and still as cute as ever.

Just as he did all that time ago, Richard said 'hello' then made himself scarce. I took Rachel to a café near the cathedral and we caught up. As excited as I was to see her, I was devastated to hear my former girlfriend's news.

She admitted she had freaked when I told her my background. She didn't know what to say, so she hid. 'You think I'm so mature, but I'm not,' she apologised. A year after leaving me, she had been raped by a French boy at a party. 'Then I knew how you felt,' she told me. 'I knew what it was like to be used. To be you.'

For a while we sat in silence and hugged. Her revelation was shocking. But we both knew there were no words to get her through her distress. It was enough for her to know that I knew how she felt. She wasn't alone. I could empathise.

I was glad I could help her. And in a way I was helped too. Meeting Rachel again was like a wake-up call for me. I got a glimpse of the future through seeing my past. She liked me, so why couldn't someone else?

I met Rosalie through my friends Stuart and Alexis in Sleaford. Going on first impressions she was as striking and individual in her own way as Rachel. Rosalie wasn't a goth, but she had just returned from a charity trip to Kenya and had had her long hair braided by the local women. I don't know what she thought of me, or whether she even noticed me among the various friends in the room, but the second time we met will stick in my memory for ever.

Stuart owned a record shop with his friend James, which meant we had a constant supply of new tracks to get stoned to. On one occasion we thought that LSD would be a more appropriate accompaniment. We were totally in the zone when Alexis arrived with Rosalie.

As only drugged-up fools can, Stuart and I tried to hide what we were up to. Unfortunately I couldn't stop laughing and he started to freak out, with my paranoia arriving shortly afterwards. 'I think you should go for a walk to calm down, don't you?' Alexis suggested. Like children, Stuart and I meekly agreed.

I was surprised when Rosalie said she fancied some fresh air too and that she'd come along. I was even more surprised when, about an hour later as the three of us walked along the riverbank, I found myself holding her hand.

When we all crashed out at Stuart's later that night, Rosalie and I shared a sofabed in the lounge. We kissed, but little more, due to the fact that another friend was asleep on another sofa a few feet away.

Just as we whispered goodnight to each other, the light in the room went on and in the doorway stood Stuart's flatmate, John. He took one look at us and exploded. 'What the fuck do you think you're doing?' he yelled. Before I could say anything, he'd picked up some plates from the table and threw them against the wall.

While Rosalie and I dived for cover under our blanket, Stuart ran into the room to see what was going on. A minute later the front door slammed and John disappeared.

'What on Earth was that about?' I asked Rosalie.

'I've no fucking idea,' she said.

It was Stuart who came up with the answer. Apparently John had got it into his head that he and Rosalie were an item. He'd told everyone, it seems, apart from Rosalie.

I was amazed that Rosalie could laugh about it so quickly, but she did, and I joined in. She impressed me a lot that night. In fact she impressed me every day over the next four years as we became boyfriend and girlfriend.

It was Rosalie who inspired me to clean up my act yet again. More important, she didn't recoil when I revealed the truth about my past.

'I don't care about before, I only care about now,' she told me. 'And if I can help you come to terms with it, I will.'

Rosalie said things to me that no one else ever had. She was everything that I had been looking for in my drug-addled state. I just hadn't realised.

'You've got to start living for you,' she told me. And she was right. I had been negative for too long. Selfishness was the only behaviour I knew. I had to put the past behind me. I had to find a direction for my life and begin to go forwards. 'You can't change your history, but you can change your future.'

I had no idea what I was going to do, but I knew how I was going to do it. And I wouldn't be alone.

'My father may have stolen the first half of my life,' I thought. 'But the second half belongs to me.'

16

I Want Custody

The forecasts for my future when I left school were the educational equivalent of a doctor giving you months to live. In the authorities' eyes I would never amount to anything. In their professional opinion, my father's words were accurate: I would never be more than 'a real loser'.

I'd believed that diagnosis for nearly ten years. 'Now I want a second opinion,' I thought.

When I first met Rosalie's family in the early 1990s, I automatically assumed they were 'posh'. I knew I didn't fit in and I guessed this was the reason. But it wasn't class that separated us. It was education.

Terry and Michelle, her dad and mum, never really accepted me as a good enough boyfriend for their beloved daughter Rosalie. Perhaps they had a point. I was the one who took her to all-night raves when they wanted her to revise for exams. She had won a place studying social anthropology at the prestigious London School of Economics, and I was a layabout dossing around in Lincoln, scraping a living from selling drugs.

On the surface we couldn't have been more different. She had the LSE; I had LSD.

She was doing something impressive with her life, taking

steps towards building a happy and successful future. I was trapped in the present, striving to forget my past and afraid of where tomorrow might take me.

While Rosalie seemed oblivious to our differences, Terry and Michelle were more judgemental. They didn't exactly make me welcome at first, but I know it wasn't personal. They were only looking out for their daughter. They didn't want me distracting from the education she'd worked so hard for. I understood, but it was hard.

With my background, I'm in no position to criticise anyone else's parents. I was barely speaking to my own. If I went over to Billinghay to see a mate, I sometimes put my head around the door and said 'hello' to Mum. She usually asked me to stay for dinner, but that meant sticking around till Dad came home. If I could avoid running into him, I would. As far as he was concerned, nothing had changed between us for years. After all, I hadn't confronted him with my realisation of what he truly was. From his point of view, he never asked me why I was so offhand with him these days. I wouldn't be surprised if he hadn't even noticed.

An emotional tie kept me in contact with my old home; I stayed in touch through habit. I can't pretend there was much love there, not from me. Rosalie, on the other hand, had a warm relationship with her folks. In their own way, they were as cool as Andy's mum. Whereas Janice preferred us kids to restrict our drug-taking to where she could check up on us, Rosalie's parents, despite their initial reservations about me, actually encouraged me to stay over at their house.

'They just want to be sure I'm all right,' Rosalie told me. 'They know we're going to sleep together anyway.'

I could see the logic. They would rather it took place in the safe environment of their home than in their car down some dodgy country lane.

During term-time they had no jurisdiction over what Rosalie got up to, and that's where I stepped in. I spent every spare moment I could in London, squeezing into her single bed at nights and hanging around with her mates. After a lifetime in the country, London intimidated me, but we did our best to make the most of it. It took a German student called Timo to really bring us out of our tourists' shells. He seemed to know absolutely everything that was going on in the city. The more subversive the movement, the more he liked it. The more underground the club, the quicker he took us there.

It was weird for me to spend so much time, voluntarily, in such an educational environment. Having opted out of my own learning career at the first opportunity, I felt like a fraud hanging around lecture theatres and libraries with my girl-friend. But I couldn't wait for Rosalie to come back home each holiday. I missed her too much when she was in London.

Rosalie could see my discomfort at being around students and went out of her way to discuss her studies with me, to invite my opinion and make me feel included. She didn't have to do that, but she did.

With Rosalie's coaxing, I felt a flicker of enjoyment somewhere inside me. A year earlier, the thought of chatting about social anthropology when I could be selling ounces in bars would have petrified me. But now I looked forward to our discussions. I found myself reading her textbooks and thinking about the subjects even when Rosalie wasn't around.

Still it never occurred to me to do anything about my new interest. Not until Rosalie suggested it.

'Why don't you get some qualifications?' she asked me one day.

'I'm too old for school,' I replied. And that was the end of it as far as I was concerned.

'You're silly,' she told me. 'You've got a lot to offer. You're a lot cleverer than you give yourself credit for.'

I thought that was simply the sort of thing girlfriends said, but Rosalie was serious. During one half-term she took me to a careers centre in Sleaford, near Lincoln. I ended up clumsily trying to explain to a middle-aged woman my hopes of tackling some sort of further education. Rather than laugh at me, the woman suggested several institutions that were currently enrolling and persuaded me to put aside my fears.

'But I'm an adult,' I told her.

'That doesn't matter.'

'And I have a criminal record.'

'We all deserve a second chance.'

With her help, I applied for a place at four adult education colleges and was selected for interview by two of them. The prospectus from Harlech College stated that it took people with little or no formal education, union members and in some circumstances ex-convicts. It sounded perfect. To my delight I was accepted to study for a diploma in General Science. The fact that I had friends in Wales meant I wouldn't be lonely if it all got too much. I couldn't wait.

Rosalie's was not the only voice encouraging me to give education another chance. The other belonged to a man called Derrick Williamson.

Derrick is a psychiatrist. I'm also proud to call him a friend. After a lifetime of trying to get by alone on a day-to-day basis, in 1993, aged twenty-three, I finally admitted I needed help from someone who wouldn't be intimidated by my past. I had so many ideas and thoughts and fears in my head that I needed to share them with someone who could help me put them into some kind of order. Also, I was very aware that I did not want to lose Rosalie by burdening her with all my problems. She seemed all right at the time, but what if she couldn't really cope with the truth as well as I hoped? Like Rachel, like Andy, like Stephen and Jim?

In the beginning I saw Derrick weekly, then every fortnight, then once a month until I set off for Harlech. Revealing to a stranger my darkest secrets was difficult at first, but Derrick's manner teased everything out of me. There was nothing I felt I could not tell him.

Some of our work was designed to encourage me to go forward with my life. Derrick was as keen for me to learn as Rosalie was. 'You're asking questions I can't answer,' he told me once. 'You should seriously consider studying psychology for yourself. You're obviously interested enough.'

The rest of our time was spent trying to make sense of the past. Why did my father abuse me? Was he homosexual? Was it all about power? Had he been abused as a child? Did he really not know he was hurting me?

Some questions I can never answer. Top of that list is: 'why?' Only one man knows the truth. But my time with Derrick was not about that man. It was about me.

Speaking to a professional who could translate some of my memories and decode the theories that I had built up over the years was worth any price. That does not mean I enjoyed all our sessions, however. There were several that left me more disturbed when I left Derrick's room than when I entered.

'Do you think your father abused anyone else?'

It was a simple question from my therapist. But unlike many of the others he posed, this one had never occurred to me. I thought about it.

'Did Dad ever abuse anyone else?' Surely not. How could he? 'I'm the one he loved,' I told Derrick. 'I'm the one he wanted to touch. I'm the one he wanted to give pleasure to. Sure, he was a fuck-up, but he abused me because he loved me.'

'Are you sure about that, Duncan?' Derrick said in his usual calm tones. 'Most abusers have more than one victim.'

Immediately I knew he was right, but for some reason I fought it. I could not accept that my father would have touched another person. He couldn't have, could he? He just couldn't have.

What was my problem? 'Am I jealous?' I questioned myself. 'Am I really jealous that someone else might have been raped by my father?'

I realised the answer was 'yes'.

It made no sense to me, but that was really how I felt. It was like being fourteen again, and realising that I had grown so accustomed to his touch, the way he told me he loved me and the times we spent alone together in the bathroom, that when the flicks finally stopped and he became distant, I missed them. As much as I hated the physical relationship we had, I actually missed the attention that went with it once it had gone.

At the time, I was too young to work out the reasons. Now, with Derrick's help, I could begin to understand my own emotions. I could appreciate how I had become conditioned to associate love with a certain kind of physical attention.

I started to allow myself to analyse my father's behaviour retrospectively. Following on from Derrick's question, I knew at once I probably wasn't the only victim. He had too many links to scout groups, football clubs and other youth organisations. He had always had a constant flow of kids doing odd jobs for him. He was like the Pied Piper of Billinghay around his yard. Kids were everywhere.

I'm ashamed to admit it, but at that moment I wasn't thinking about the pain he may have imposed on other innocent lives. I was concentrating on the sense of rejection that was welling up inside me. 'He didn't love me at all, did he?' I asked Derrick. 'It was all lies to keep me quiet.'

Every time I thought my father could not sink lower in my estimation, he achieved it. I promised myself I would do something about it when I finished my college course. 'He's not going to get away with it for ever,' I pledged.

The academic opportunities offered to me by Harlech were incredible. But I benefited in other ways that I could not have predicted.

Although I was miles away from Rosalie, the new life and new set-up went some way to take my mind off the recent epiphanies I'd achieved with Derrick's help.

If I was worried about feeling inadequate or 'stupid' among the other students, I quickly learned I had nothing to fear on that score. The rest of the class comprised people from all walks of life and many different backgrounds. I was in a much healthier mental state than several of them. One chap committed suicide shortly after the final term kicked off. He was obviously in a bad way in his life. Like me, he'd seen Harlech as his last chance at redemption. For him, it proved a step too far, too soon.

I am sorry I could not help him. I know how it feels to be in that position. To actually wake up one day and believe, 'I would be better off dead.'

He wasn't the only one with problems. Some students, I discovered, had been through experiences similar to mine. I never dreamed I would find so many like-minded people in one room. Within a few weeks of the class starting, I found myself comfortable telling near strangers about my past. And it felt good. It felt very good indeed.

My openness, learned through so many sessions with Derrick, encouraged others to step forwards. Several people approached me with their stories. Others shared their scarred memories with the whole class.

On one occasion, I had a conversation with a rapist. He had served a prison sentence for his crime and was trying to make a new life. I commend anyone who wants to put their past behind them. But as I spoke to him, I sensed he did not really appreciate the severity of his crime. He knew he had been bad, because he had been arrested and punished. But what was going on in his mind? Why did he speak as though he were the victim? 'It's not my place to judge him,' I thought, 'but I need him to understand. From the point of view of someone who has been abused, he needs to understand.'

I made that man cry. Later he thanked me for being honest with him.

A few weeks later a woman in her forties approached me and said she had been raped by her father and brothers. We were not really friends as such, but she said that after hearing me talk, she had felt able to disclose her story to me. 'You're the first person I've ever told,' she said.

That one sentence was worth more to me than any qualification I could ever earn.

I enjoyed my role as an ad hoc counsellor. For the first time in my life I felt as if I was giving something back, instead of just taking. I'd never had anything to give before. Apart from drugs.

Being everyone's friend did not score me any extra marks on my coursework, however. If I'm honest, the academic side of things was tougher than I expected. My brain hadn't been used in that way for so long, it had almost rusted up.

Harlech's policy was to ease us all in as gently as possible. During the first weeks we only had to produce 500-word reports. By the end of the year we were churning out university-length essays.

Deadlines were a problem for me. I got through the classes OK, and once I overcame my feeling of being in an alien environment, I could hold my own in most discussions with the tutors, confident for the first time in my life that my opinions were valid. But discipline and me parted company years ago. It didn't help that there always seemed to be a great party to go to the day before we were due to deliver our work.

The social side of college life was every bit as important to me as the academic part. I seemed to have invites coming from every direction, and with my new confidence I tried to take up as many as I could. When Rosalie came to visit, she couldn't believe the transformation in my personality.

I never worked well under pressure. The prospect of coming up with a 1,500-word essay overnight usually struck fear into me. Drugs had got me through times of stress in the past – whole years, in fact – and they did again now. When I wasn't actually in class I spent a lot of time tripping on ecstasy. I wasn't alone – the whole place was drowning in the stuff.

I soon discovered opportunities to deal the odd pack of pills here and there. As far as my own consumption was concerned, however, I tried to be more grown-up. If I could focus on getting high for pleasure, rather than for escape from issues I was struggling to cope with, that was OK. I was lucky enough to have accommodation in a three-storey Welsh cottage on a hillside in Llys Branwen, about five minutes' walk away from the college. Sitting at the window, spliff in hand and gazing at the beautiful view of Harlech Bay below, was almost like therapy in itself.

After each term ended, I came home from Wales to stay with Rosalie. My mum occasionally suggested I stop over with them, but I never entertained the idea. I did, at her suggestion, let my father drive me back to college each term, however.

Why did I still talk to him? It's hard to answer. The main reason on these occasions was because he could do something for me. Most of my life he had used me. I had been the victim. Making him do something for me for a change, without getting anything in return, seemed strangely tempting. Even though it was such a small thing compared to what he'd taken from me, I couldn't resist going for it. I'd spent years hiding my true feelings in front of him, so from that point a few hours in a van weren't going to kill me. Not if I felt I was in control for once.

I also wanted to see if I could actually bear to be in my father's company. Before my sessions with Derrick, I couldn't think of Dad without feelings of rage, resentment and loathing flooding my thoughts. I wanted to discover, as time went on, whether my months of therapy were altering my view of my abuser. We hadn't long left Billinghay at the start of my final term when I realised that they were. As we drove along the M4 that day I admitted to myself that I didn't really care about my father any more. That was why I could tolerate being in his company now. I wasn't driven by rage any more. My hatred had become pity. And even that was in short supply.

Dad never hung around when we got to Harlech, and that final time was no different. I thanked him for the lift, made perfunctory conversation and didn't look back as he pulled away.

It was the last time I would see him for ten years.

My last term at Harlech was very eventful. Two bits of news from home completely took my breath away. The first came in a phone call from Dad. He rang to tell me his firm had gone bankrupt. 'We'll be all right, son,' he assured me. 'I'll turn things around.' The worst thing about going bust was that he was obliged to sell the family home to pay off his business debts. If he had taken his accountant's advice and registered as a limited company then he would have been covered. My mother would still have had a house after twenty-seven years of marriage.

After so many years of holding back my true emotions in front of him, I finally exploded. I couldn't hide the disgust in my voice as I pointed out how pathetic he had been to destroy everything my mother had worked towards during their life together.

It was a cathartic moment in my life, and one I wish I had experienced years earlier. All the anger I had bottled up because of what he had done to me came pouring out. I may not have had the strength to confront him over what he'd subjected me to, but faced with him destroying my mother's life I felt suddenly free of inhibitions. I was doing this for her – for his wife, my mother – and I didn't hold back.

At the end of the call I was drained emotionally. But I hope I achieved something on my mother's behalf. I hope I made him appreciate the pain he had caused her.

From my point of view, that call was memorable for another reason. It was the last time I would ever speak to my father.

The second piece of news was even more dramatic. Mum rang me and announced, 'I'm getting a divorce.' She put it down to the fact that he had been stupid with their money and lost her home. That's what she was telling everyone. But I knew there was another reason – because I had given it to her.

The trip to Harlech with my father a few weeks earlier had crystallised the feelings in my mind. I was amazed at how little I felt for him. 'I've got nothing to fear from you any more,' I thought.

With that in my mind, I had picked up the phone and made the most difficult call of my life. During the next few minutes, I told my mother everything.

I wasn't surprised by her reaction, although I still took it badly. She refused to believe what I was saying – she just couldn't take it in.

I tried my best to remain calm. 'Ask Jo,' I said. 'Ask her about Dad.'

I don't know what inspired me to think of telling her to ask my sister. It wasn't premeditated. Jo and I had never spoken about Dad. I'd never told her anything about what he did to me.

A short while later my mother rang back. My hunch was right and Jo had corroborated my story. Years ago she had told Mum, 'Daddy is hurting Duncan in the bathroom', and Mum hadn't believed her. I was furious when I heard this.

'You mean, she told you and you did nothing about it?' I shouted into the phone.

'No, I didn't understand what she meant,' my mother explained. 'She was a kid. I thought she'd heard you moaning about not showering. I'm so sorry.'

I struggled to comprehend the news. My sister had suspected something bad was going on and had told Mum and Mum just hadn't understood her.

I came off the phone shell-shocked. Just when I thought my world could tear no further apart, it had managed it. I needed a spliff. I needed Rosalie and I needed Derrick.

Years later I spoke to my mother about this conversation. She remembered it as vividly as I did. I learned that I was not the only one distraught by the revelations of that day. But whereas my thoughts had turned to cannabis, hers had turned to violence. I was shocked by her story.

'When I went to bed that night,' she told me, 'I took a kitchen knife upstairs with me. Your father was already in bed, snoring. I stood over him and said under my breath,

"So this is what a paedophile looks like. I bloody married one." '

My mother never swore. This was important.

'But I couldn't do it. I couldn't stab him. I wanted to so much but I didn't have the courage.'

Part of me wished she had. But then her life would have been ruined even more by him. She would have sunk to his level. And he would have died without even being told why.

I didn't know if I would ever be confident enough to tell him what he was. I didn't know if my mother would, or my sister. But I had to hope that he would be made to pay some time. I had to believe that he would not get away with it for ever.

But that was for the future. Somehow I also needed to find time for the small matter of passing my course.

My mother initiated divorce proceedings later that year. My dad did not oppose the move. His only comment was this: 'I'll give you your divorce, but I want custody of the kids.'

I was twenty-four; my sister was twenty-eight.

'What on Earth is he thinking?' I asked my mother, but she was as mystified as me. 'Is he really that deluded?' I said.

My own question took me by surprise. Over the years I had decided my father was selfish, evil, domineering – but never mad. Was I wrong? It was possible. But his words seemed to me to be the knee-jerk reaction of a destroyed man who was desperately trying to maintain control. He had lost his business, his home and now his wife. It was typical of him to lash out and try to threaten my mother with taking the only thing she had left – her kids. It was typical of him to think he knew more than anyone else.

And it was typical of him not to realise that I would rather die than live with him ever again.

17

You'll Know When You're Ready

If you believe the tabloid press in the UK, most qualifications are not worth the paper they're printed on. I disagree. When I was awarded a diploma in General Science from Harlech College, it showed to the world I didn't have to be a 'waster', a 'useless druggie' or a 'scumbag'. That was a lifestyle I had been forced into by circumstance. But there was more to me than the frightened man running away from his past, even if I hadn't believed it.

I had given up on myself long ago. Luckily for me, Rosalie and her family, Derrick Williamson and good friends like Richard and Dave never did. I owe them all so much.

The qualification in General Science was just the beginning. With Derrick's words still fresh in my ears – 'you should study this subject' – I signed up for a full degree course in psychotherapy at Worcester College of Higher Education.

After the impressive camaraderie at Harlech it was a shock to the system when I turned up on day one. In Wales, we were all adults who'd been through the wringer and emerged the other side. There was an unspoken bond between us. In Worcester I stuck out like a sore thumb. I was what is known as a 'mature' student. Virtually everyone else was a fresh-faced kid.

Despite the age gap I did my best to fit in. But even though I had fun, I needed more than buddies for a boozy night out. There was no one I felt comfortable coming clean with about my background. After the relief of Harlech it was a depressing blow to have to hide my past once again.

Supporting myself was just as difficult. I had won funding to cover my place at college, but living costs and textbooks had to be paid for somehow. I was determined to make a go of my second chance at an education, but selling drugs was the only thing close to a long-term career I had known. A college campus presents an endless queue of customers, and I admit I took advantage of their innocence to make a decent return on each deal.

The more time went by, however, the angrier I got with myself for not being able to break out of my old patterns. Not only was I selling, but I was also using too much and my work was suffering. Something had to give. 'Calm down or get off the course,' I lectured myself. 'If you throw it away now, you'll just prove all the doubters right.' Worse, I'd prove my father right.

'I'm not a loser,' I thought. 'I know that now.'

I decided to make changes. I stopped dealing and managed to get a part-time job that didn't impact too much on my studies. Not only had selling weed been lucrative, but the hours were good. Still, if I was serious about this I had to make the effort. The last rave I went to, at the Rocket Club in Holloway Road, London, in 1996, also marked the last time I took LSD.

That was a big concession for me. My drug of choice has

always been cannabis. But after that it was ecstasy, LSD, speed and coke. I'd rather smoke than snort or swallow. But you take what's around. Giving up everything would be hard, since I owed it so much, since I had sheltered under its protective umbrella for so long. But I had to start somewhere. One step at a time.

Another change in my life happened soon after. Rosalie and I were aware that we had been growing apart over recent months. It was a gradual process. I probably wasn't the same guy she'd met four years earlier, and we'd both matured and experienced so much during our time together. We had a tearful conversation in which we both admitted how much we loved each other but that it was probably for the best if we separated, and then we said goodbye. I will always be grateful for the help she gave me and the confidence she instilled in me to improve my life.

A short while later I met Nicola, whose family lived in South Wales. We immediately hit it off and became lovers as well as friends. I wonder sometimes how she would have liked the 'old' me. The man she fell in love with was a nose-to-the-grindstone student whose drug consumption was no more than average among undergraduates.

One of the modules I chose to take was Abnormal Psychology, in which we studied minority sexualities. Many of them have become popular underground movements and have acquired a kitsch, but acceptable profile in the mass media. Traits like exhibitionism, fetishism, frotteurism, sadism, masochism and voyeurism, for example. One category interested me above all: it was paedophilia, and it was the reason I took the course. I wanted to understand my abuser. I wanted to get into his mind.

I discovered little about my father, but I did learn that I was one of the lucky ones. Like so many paedophiles he had expressed signs of being obsessed with controlling others, of being sexually immature and emotionally stunted, of seeing people as possessions and little more than a means to his sexual ends. But ten years of abuse, wanking Dad three times a week and being raped when it suited him was a light sexual sentence compared to some of the case studies we looked at. My heart grieves for all victims, but the grotesque behaviour endured by some defies belief.

I did get beaten, but not often or badly. I didn't get locked in cupboards. I didn't get starved, my face rubbed in shit, or forced to sleep in a piss-soaked bed night after night. There are many who did.

Driven to hide my 'real' self from the majority of my fellow students, I leaned more than I would have liked on my girlfriend. One of the reasons I liked her was her great Welsh accent. I also liked her attitude, even though it frustrated the hell out of me. Nicola was happy-go-lucky. For about a year she refused to acknowledge we were a couple. We made love together, went on dates and slept in each other's homes, but she wouldn't hold my hand in public, let alone kiss or hug me when friends were around.

When I met her parents, I realised where she got her free spirit from.

Nicola's dad, Roger, is an amazing man. I learned a lot about life from him, and about people. Together with Dave, he is a father figure every bit as perfect as my real father was flawed.

Nicola consulted her father on pretty much everything. She

eventually asked him, 'Should I let Duncan date me or not?' I owe him a lot for saying 'yes'.

Nicola's mum, Sheila, is equally impressive and I looked forward to the times we'd visit, and the compulsory trip down the local pub after dinner. Then it was back to their house for a nightcap of malt whisky and talking until the cows came home.

I remember vividly telling Roger about my family. The girls had gone to bed and he disappeared into the kitchen and returned with two glasses of ice. 'You'll like this,' he said, and carefully poured generous measures of Bushmills into each one.

He sat and listened intently while I recounted my background. With great sensitivity he then helped me weigh up the option of going to the police.

'I wouldn't stand a chance in a courtroom,' I said. 'The lawyers would tear me to shreds.'

'Maybe now,' Roger said. 'But it won't always be like this. You'll know when you're ready.'

When Dad's business went belly-up, the biggest loser was Mum. Through no fault of her own she was suddenly homeless at fifty-seven. When the divorce went through she was awarded £14,000 from a lifetime's investment in a house worth more than six times that. Dad went straight on to benefits and into rented accommodation.

With the settlement and some savings she scraped together, Mum managed to buy a new place and exists today on a state pension. In the space of a few months she went from a large, three-bedroom detached house with land to a two-up, two-down terrace with a small yard. My father not only took away my childhood. Through his financial ineptitude, he also stole my mother's golden years.

For the first time in my life, I found myself getting along with my mother. I don't know if it was a feeling of solidarity as two victims of my father's actions, or whether it was just because we weren't both in temperamental moods because of the shadow of his presence, but I found myself opening up to her and, to a certain extent, her to me.

I phoned her regularly and we'd talk for hours at a time about Dad and the effect he had had on me. We were both angry at how he had, as she put it, 'got away with everything while the rest of us suffered'. She discussed her own life in a very businesslike way, not emotionally at all. This happened and then this, she would say. She never expressed regret or made excuses. I think my mother must have blocked out a lot of the reality going on around her. I am sad that we couldn't have helped each other at the time.

Over time I began to pity her life more and more. 'If I can do something to put things right, to make him pay, I will,' I promised myself.

When I graduated from Worcester with a 2:ii in Psychology I was surprised at my mother's reaction. 'I'm coming to see your graduation ceremony,' she told me. 'I've already bought my hat.'

'What ceremony?' I said. 'I can't be bothered going. I've got my certificate, that's all I need. I haven't got money to waste on getting dressed up for a day.'

That's where she surprised me. 'I'll pay,' she said. 'You've got to go. It wouldn't be right not to.'

Lack of money wasn't the only reason I didn't care about the passing-out parade. Even though I had had many other things distracting me over the last three years, I was still disappointed to earn only a 2:ii.

It was a pretty good day, all things considered. Mum caught the train from Grantham, and Nicola and I played hosts as we gave her the tour of the city.

When all the photographs had been taken, hands shaken and certificates handed over, my mother came over and said, 'I'm proud of you, son. You may not be much but you're mine and I'm proud of you.'

I think she was trying to be nice. As usual it came out like a back-handed compliment, but I let it go.

'It's not her fault,' I rationalised. 'Anyone would be screwed if they lived with that bastard for so long.' I was in the mood to be charitable. The black sheep, crook and drug addict had just climbed another rung up the ladder.

Unfortunately my good mood soon evaporated. The point of getting a degree is to get work. But I could not find a job for love nor money.

For two years I searched for the answer to the question 'Where will my degree take me?'. During that time Nicola and I stayed in Worcester and survived on myriad dead-end jobs. For a while I earned good money in a freezer factory, but it reminded me too much of working for Dad.

I thought I had found my niche when I was invited to join the staff at a special needs school in the Midlands. After a couple of months I was forced to resign for reporting an instance of physical child abuse directly to the police rather than going through the proper channels at the school. Even though that episode upset me, I realised that working in education was in my blood. Nicola and I registered for positions teaching English as a foreign language, and over the next few years we enjoyed stints working with the vast international populations in Winchester, Jersey and Bournemouth.

I was working at St Alfred's College in Winchester when I met a seventeen-year-old Japanese girl who spoke so beautifully about her country and the need there for teachers that I couldn't wait for the next phase of my life with Nicola to begin.

'Finally I know where my degree can take me,' I thought. 'Japan.'

I turned thirty in 2000. It was a momentous time for contrasting reasons. On the one hand I was about to embark on the experience of a lifetime in a foreign culture. On the other I could not escape my past. Every day, when I looked in the mirror, I saw the face of my tormentor staring back at me.

Everyone says I look like my father. The older I get, the more I grow into his physical replica. It is my curse. I look like him, I sound like him and I have many of the same experiences as him.

But I am not him. I won't let my life take the shape that his did.

In Billinghay, in Lincoln and various points around the UK I get stopped by people who know me through my father. It upsets me every time. In Japan I had the chance to create my own history without the baggage.

The JET teaching programme reflects the pinnacle of international teaching. I was thrilled to be accepted, and with something which only 5 per cent of applicants achieve: my first-choice location.

My selection, from the available sites, was Nagano, Okinawa and Hokkaido. I chose them because I wanted to expose myself, not only to Japan, but to as many other new experiences as I could, including winter sports.

In Europe skiing is the preserve of the rich. In Japan I joined that rarefied world at a fraction of the cost. It was not cheap, but with sacrifices it was do-able.

I flew with Nicola to Tokyo, but there we parted. She hadn't been so lucky with her choice, although her post in Kofu was easily reachable from my base in Nagano. We both inherited company cars from our predecessors and put them to good use over the next few months. In many ways we had the best of both worlds. By chance we were forced to socialise with strangers and make friends in our respective areas, but every weekend we got to see each other.

I was stationed at the Shiojiri Shi Prefectural Education Centre, a city office responsible for the delivery of a county-wide education programme in line with the government's curriculum. I also worked at an academic high school and a lower-level agricultural technical college.

The work was varied and straightforward. I quickly got into the routine and, compared with anything I experienced in the UK, it was easy money. My rent was subsidised, just 35 quid a month for a one-bedroom flat, and from a monthly salary of £1,500 I had plenty to spare to enjoy the local culture.

There were eight different ski resorts within an hour of my house, so I started saving as soon as I got there. Nicola and I had both mastered surfing and body-boarding during our university days. We couldn't wait to learn snowboarding.

We hit the slopes as soon as the first snow fell in the second week of November. I spent the majority of the first day on my back and pulled muscles I didn't know I had, but by the end of the second day I could get from A to B without hitting anyone else.

Any chance I got, I took off for the mountains. I faked more than one illness to get away. It became my new addiction. I lived a very frugal life, just so I could go boarding at the weekend. Every weekend.

I had never had a healthy passion before. Not unless you counted drugs. I was in love with snowboarding. It took me to new highs, buzzed me up in a way I had never imagined without chemical help.

By contrast, the ex-pat social scene down in the cities was awash with alcoholics and out-of-shape Englishmen drinking to obliterate their personal problems. As someone who has been there, I couldn't judge them. But as someone who has emerged the other side, I just wanted to shake them all. 'You've got so much to live for,' I wanted to shout.

While the entire ex-pat scene revolved around drinking and getting totally shit-faced, everyone looked down on me if I said, 'I really fancy a spliff.' In Japan possession carries a heavy jail sentence. It doesn't do to encourage that sort of talk, I soon learned.

I tried to make Japanese friends, but this is easier said than done. My best friends from that time are Big Steve and Bushy Paul, both of whom are very English.

Japan is a country of such contrasts, from huge warehouse parties to quaint little villages where the kids have never seen a white man's face before. Far from making friends among the locals, I experienced small children crying when they saw me and hiding behind their mum. Even with my basic grasp of Japanese I understood when she explained, 'With your white skin you look like a ghost to my two-year-old son.'

The only people I liked and who liked me were my students. Although separated by thousands of miles geographically and hundreds of years culturally, we had a lot in common. Several of them had personal problems that I tried to help with. One confided in me how she witnessed her father beat her mother after drinking. She left the school and we stayed in touch and became friends. Years later she was sexually assaulted in a nightclub in Tokyo. She was very upset and blamed herself. I told her my problems because I wanted her to know that she wasn't alone, and to make sure she understood that it wasn't her fault.

'That's why you understood my feelings so well,' she said. 'You knew what I was feeling.'

My snowboarding obsession met its match on Mount Noriku Dake in Nagano Ken. I don't remember what happened. My board slipped from under me and the next thing I recall is being dumped on my back in the hard snow. I spent three months in hospital and had to have two operations, one of five hours and another of one hour – during which I had to be conscious. As a result of the fall, my left leg showed signs of having withered. Before the surgery I had to sign a disclaimer. I had no choice. The medics said I could never walk again without the operations.

Not for the first time, I had a chance in the sanitised environs of a hospital to reflect on my life. Physically my body was struggling, but mentally I got stronger every day, and I soon worked out the next step in my life. I decided that as soon as I was declared fit, I would return to England to take the exams required to enter the mainstream of the British education profession. If I could prevent one pupil from going down the reckless path I had followed, I would be happy.

My desire to help kids was tested sooner than I expected. Two days after I landed back in the UK, fully recuperated from my ordeal, I took a stroll through Grantham. A sight in front of me took my breath away. There, large as life, was my father. Walking with him was a young boy with dark hair. They were holding hands and laughing, oblivious to on-lookers.

Perhaps other passers-by that day assumed the scene being played out involved a child and his doting grandfather. I knew that wasn't true. I still shudder to recall how my father virtually walked into me but didn't recognise his own son. He was too engrossed in his young companion. To this day I don't know who the boy was. But I was finally ready to act. I knew I had to do something for him.

But what?

The answer was something I wish I'd done years ago. I would challenge my father. I would make him pay for what he did to me, and I would ensure he never harmed another child again. I would get myself ready, mentally and physically, and I would take him on in court.

As the thought entered my mind I knew I was consigning myself to a year, possibly two, of struggle, pain and upheaval. But whatever the price, I would pay it. Whatever the sacrifice, I would make it.

My father had to be brought to justice.

In September 2003 I started a two-year PGCE degree course at St Martin's College, Lancaster. I wanted to have a secure profession under my belt before I made my next move. Being qualified to teach in the UK within the mainstream education sector seemed the best idea.

A lot of things changed for me that year. Sadly, Nicola and I split up after six or seven great years (depending on whether she was counting or I was). Two new friends, Big Dave and Laura, started to play large parts in my life. I quit drinking, took the choice to be celibate for a year and embarked on a campaign of physical fitness. Through regular gym work and swimming I went from sixteen stone to eleven.

During my study periods and evenings I dedicated a lot of reading time to exploring law texts. I wanted to know my options.

The next part of my plan came into place at the end of the academic year. It was important to me psychologically that I was better prepared than my father in every way. I wanted to experience more of the world and explore new cultures, to recharge my batteries before I went toe to toe with the man who had tried to ruin my life.

In June I set off on a trip to Cambodia and Thailand. Both countries introduced me to wonders I had never dreamed of. More important, I met a person who would change my life for ever.

The Swiss Park Hotel in Bangkok would normally be a little out of my league, but after the dust and poverty of Cambodia I felt ready for a bit of luxury. It cost $20 a night. Luxury comes cheap in Thailand.

On my second morning I was walking to reception to hand my key in for the day when I noticed a young woman about to do the same thing. I could tell from her mannerisms and body language that she was Japanese.

'Ohaiyo Gozaimasu,' I said, as our eyes met.

My words were a simple 'good morning', but her face lit up and she rattled off a flurry of high-speed words in reply. I managed to work out the first few – 'Oh! You can speak Japanese – that's good . . .' but after that I was lost and I had to admit it.

'We can speak English if you prefer?' she said, pleased that I had at least tried to speak her mother tongue.

Her name was Chie. Like me, she was travelling alone, so we decided to do a spot of sightseeing together. For the five days of her stay we spent every waking moment together. We only parted company to go to bed.

Apart from her beauty, the thing that struck me about Chie was her personality. She was so open, honest and kind, yet very shrewd and intelligent.

She also had a good sense of humour. This came in very useful as we realised that the majority of people who saw us together assumed she was a Thai prostitute and I was her client. I'm afraid I wasn't the only western guy with an attractive Asian girl on my arm. But were those other men falling in love with their companions, as I was?

On Chie's last day in Thailand I decided to make my feelings known. We had just had a wonderful day together and as we stood on the Koa Sarn Road, I leant down to kiss her. Caught off guard, she turned slightly and my lips landed on the top of her head. I don't know which of us was more embarrassed. Chie responded first. She jumped into the next cab that passed and disappeared into the night.

'Well, you screwed that one up,' I told myself. 'Another one bites the dust.'

The next few days were miserable. Thailand seemed very

empty without Chie. I was tormented by the idea of what might have been. To cheer myself up I decided to get in touch with some of my friends back home. When I checked my e-mails I couldn't believe my eyes. There in my inbox was a message from Chie. She thanked me for a wonderful time and made me laugh as much in writing as she had in person. She said she had never been treated with such courtesy and respect by a man before. This made me so proud, but also a little sad, as it seemed to imply that she had suffered in the past. Little did she know that I had spent five days trying to pluck up the courage to kiss her.

I couldn't wait to see her again.

I returned to the UK alone in August 2004, refreshed and energised for what lay ahead. The pieces were all in place in my mind. I was ready mentally, and physically I had never been fitter. On 16 August I walked into Grantham police station and reported my father as a child abuser and paedophile.

On 11 November 2004, Clifford John Fairhurst was arrested by Lincolnshire Police and charged with 35 counts of sexual abuse. He was immediately bailed and left the police station the same day.

Wheels were turning. People were taking notice. I had started a process called 'Justice' that was now out of my hands.

So why did I feel that I was the one on trial?

18

We Do Things Differently Here

I thought long and hard before I decided to press charges against my father. Was I prepared to take on that much work? Could I cope with it at the same time as trying to study or work? What effect would it have on our family?

Even though I had only known her a few months, Chie became my rock. We only corresponded by e-mail at first, but there was an intensity and honesty in our talk that I had never experienced before. In an early message I told her about a friend of mine who was embarking on a prosecution against his father. But in October 2004 she flew over to England for one week and I decided to risk telling her the truth. We went for a drive in the Lake District, parked on top of a hill and I told her straight. She listened attentively then said, 'You don't have to say any more. I knew you were talking about your own life in the e-mail. Whatever I can do to support you, I will. I love you.'

Chie's visit confirmed in both our minds that we had a future together. What we felt for each other in Thailand had not been a holiday romance. After she left, our e-mailing reached frenetic levels. The messages also became very passionate.

During one exchange I tested my Japanese again and typed, 'Kekkon shite-kureru?'

The words meant 'Will you marry me?'. Her reply was instant but inconclusive: 'I'm shocked!' she wrote. 'That's no answer,' I thought. Panicking, I told her not to mention it until we met again.

During another round of messages, I confided to Chie my fears about the workload facing me. Apart from wanting to spend every moment with her, I was about to start the second year of my teacher training course at Lancaster University. With a training grant and a student loan I could just about scrape by financially, but I wasn't sure how I would fit in all the work. 'I was abused regularly for ten years,' I explained. 'It could take months for the police to process everything I have to say. For all I know, I might have to work closely with them until the trial.' Putting myself and Chie first, I was genuinely worried. I wondered whether I would really have time to give the police everything they needed.

The answer, sadly, was yes. What the police wanted from me, I could have fitted in during a long lunch break.

I spent twenty years getting over the pain my father inflicted on me. Half of that time I devoted to improving myself, getting ready physically and mentally to take on the legal system. In ten years I had worked out a lot of things I wanted to say. A lot of things I needed to say.

The police gave me ninety minutes of their time.

It had not for one moment occurred to me that I would struggle to get the police interested in my story. I knew that a prosecution would be difficult, but I thought at least I would have the backing of the law. I never thought they would be the ones I had to fight.

My problems started from the moment I entered Grantham police station. I didn't even get shown into a proper reception area. There were no chairs, no desk, just a passage between the door and a small window where a frazzled woman was batting away enquiries. It was like queuing at the meat counter at Lo-Cost. I was surrounded by drunks and unpleasant characters shouting, swearing and jostling for attention.

Eventually I reached the front of the line. 'May I help you, sir?' the receptionist asked.

'Can I speak to someone about a matter of child protection, please?'

'Please tell me the nature of the complaint.'

'I'd rather speak to someone in private.'

'I'm sorry, sir, we don't have the room. If you'd like to tell me your complaint . . .'

I stopped her there. There were three men stinking of booze hovering within feet of me. They could hear my every word. I did not go there to be public entertainment.

I insisted on seeing somebody in private and I was given an appointment for two days' time.

I felt so traumatised that I seriously wondered whether I could face going back.

Two days later I had a change of heart. I took a deep breath and entered the station again. My meeting was with DC Kevin Gooch. He took me to what looked like a refurbished cell, about ten feet by six, with a tiny window, bare electric light, two chairs and one desk.

I was given enough time to outline my allegations and name my abuser. Then I was informed that the Grantham Child Protection Unit was very busy and given another date on which to return.

For the second time in a week I felt my confidence pop like a balloon.

Finally I returned and was given the full weight of DC Gooch's attention for an hour and a half (apart from the times he stopped to answer the phone before taking it off the hook).

The officer was very businesslike in his approach. He wanted me to give a statement, but it had to fit into the accepted grid.

'Please only speak about incidents where you can remember where it happened and when,' he instructed me. 'Include details of what led up to the event, the event itself and any repercussions such as injuries sustained by yourself.'

'This is very difficult for me,' I said. 'I was so young, there were so many incidents. The dates and places blur into one after a while.'

'We need to be very precise for the courts,' he said. 'If you can't remember it clearly, leave it out.'

I told him about the first time I recalled, when I was six. I recounted the time when I was promised I would be meeting Geoff Capes. I also volunteered the names of sixteen people I considered might have been at risk from my father when I was growing up, as well as the names of several friends of Dad's, such as Frank Dexter, whom I considered likely to have abused children. After ninety minutes of harrowing reminiscences, punctuated by questions such as 'When was this?', 'Did he say anything to you?' or 'Are you sure it happened like that?', DC Gooch looked at his notes and said, 'I think we have enough now.'

The officer trotted through a few procedures. He would arrange for me to speak to someone from Victim Support.

'You can't have counselling because the defence barrister will play upon that and make out you're an unstable witness,' he said.

'I won't require therapy,' I assured him, but I did take up the offer to meet the Victim Support officer, whose first task it seemed was to give me emotional support. I again explained that I was fine. 'But please contact my mother and sister,' I said. 'They need help more than I do.'

A fortnight after my first visit I returned to the police station to sign the prepared statement. It contained several mistakes, which DC Gooch blamed on the typist.

More important, I was informed that since the crimes took place in Billinghay, he would be handing over the file to the Sleaford district station.

Two days after this interview I returned to Lancaster University for the second and final year of my PGCE course. I said I was happy to come back for further interviews at any time. I was never asked.

DC Alison Smith called me during that term to announce she was the new investigating officer. She rang back later to inform me my father had been arrested.

'I've done it!' I thought. 'I've got him put away. It's all been worth it.'

It didn't work like that. My father admitted eight of the thirty-five charges immediately, which I was amazed at, but rather than being locked up until his trial, he was released on bail pending an appearance at the magistrates court.

'If he's admitted he's guilty, if he's admitted he abuses children, how can he be allowed to roam the streets?' I asked myself.

It was at this stage that I began to feel uncomfortable about what was going on. Was it my fault? Had I not given enough information to the authorities?

In November I got a call from Mum to say that Dad hadn't turned up for his magistrates court appearance and that a warrant had been issued for his arrest that day. She called back later to say the police 'had sent the boys round'. They discovered my father unconscious in his council house, apparently the victim of an overdose of paracetamol and Jack Daniel's whiskey.

I'd wished him dead many times in the last few years. But I didn't want him to die now, not without my day in court. Suicide was the coward's way out.

Although my father had admitted eight of the thirty-five police charges against him, his decision to try to kill himself, I felt, was an even more telling admission of guilt. Dad was taken to Grantham hospital before being moved to the renal care unit of the Leicester Royal Infirmary. As Christmas approached, my family badgered the police for information. Would his liver and kidneys survive? When would he be released? Would he go straight into police custody?

Meanwhile my own health was beginning to suffer. An old back complaint flared up again and I was admitted to Lancaster A&E. I had three outpatient procedures and three months of physiotherapy. It was painful and I worried that I wouldn't ever be cured. But that was not the worst of it. During the whole period I was unable to attend college, and eventually it was noted. I was informed that my teacher training grant, which I received in monthly instalments, would be frozen. My place was also effectively scrapped and I was bumped back into the following year's intake.

'The timing couldn't be worse,' I thought. 'My body's

falling apart, I need to be strong for my family, and the man I'm trying to prosecute still isn't in prison.'

With my back problems, getting a job was not easy and, because in the eyes of the authorities I was still technically a student, benefits were not available to me. On top of that, with my place at university disappearing, I was technically homeless as well. My mother offered to put me up, but like the rest of us, she had enough on her plate with the impending court case. I couldn't add to her burden by expecting her to nurse me.

I could only think of one option to get me out of the mess. For the first time in five years I started dealing in drugs again.

'I've got no choice,' I promised myself. 'It's only temporary.' But I knew that if I wasn't careful, my old lifestyle would soon creep up on me.

During my recuperation DC Smith revealed that the police had found a suicide note next to Dad's slumped body. I was glad in a perverse way. In this document he would surely say he was sorry. I couldn't wait to see it. Unfortunately I was told that it remained my father's property unless he died. Then it could be opened.

Dad pulled through and was remanded into custody on 24 December.

It was the best Christmas present I could have asked for. As I prepared to celebrate I received another call from the police. Yes, my father had been remanded, they said, but he had later been released into a relative's custody.

She had several grandchildren. I could not believe she would invite an admitted paedophile into her home where minors could be present.

'Something's not right,' I told Chie. 'The police are handling it all wrong.'

I couldn't get past the idea that every day my father remained free, another child was at risk. From my psychology training I was aware that people under pressure act in extreme and surprising ways. He had already attempted suicide. But what if he took out his frustration on others? If one more innocent suffered at his hands because the police had not kept him in custody, I don't think I could have forgiven myself. I had to keep on top of progress. I had to make sure every avenue was explored.

As far as I could see, however, relatively little action was being taken in response to the information I had handed over to the police. There were sixteen names of other possible victims – all of them boys I had seen working or playing with my father at his yard over the years. What if those lads hadn't been able to get over their problems in the way I had? What if the police getting in touch meant the difference between giving up or getting stronger? Or what if my father's defence team successfully convinced a jury that I was lying – surely the police would want as many witnesses as possible?

Even more important were the leads I had suggested regarding those associates of my father who might have abused children too. It takes a lot to inform the authorities that you think a person might be a paedophile. It's not a decision I took lightly, and I wanted it followed up. Other innocent people could be hurt.

I decided to do something about it. The Citizens Advice Bureau advised me that I could not expect any outside legal advice. If I turned to the media it could have an adverse effect on the police's case, and so I focused my energies on intervention from a higher office.

I found a supporter in my local MP, Hilton Dawson. First

of all, he helped sort out my finances. Lancaster handed over the withheld portions of my training grant. Hilton also helped arrange for a hardship grant payable to those incapacitated. The money only covered 60 per cent of my debts, but it was a start. I could at least resist the financial lure of drugs.

Hilton also contacted the Home Office on my behalf and the office of Baroness Scotland QC looked into my complaint against Lincolnshire Police. She then wrote to me and assured me that I was being treated fairly. 'May I suggest if you have any further enquiries that you contact one of the police officers.'

My jaw dropped. I could not believe what I was reading. Baroness Scotland's idea of investigating was to call the very people I had a problem with and ask them to look into it.

With my education stalling and the legal procedure seemingly falling apart, it was only the thought of Chie's next visit which kept me going. The content of our e-mails reached fever pitch in the weeks leading up to the big day, and eventually I picked her up from Heathrow Airport on 10 February 2005 – coincidentally my father's birthday. Because her flight was delayed, we spent the night in a hotel just outside Oxford before making the journey up to Lancaster the next day.

I remember us lying on our fronts side by side and watching the late BBC news. Trying to be cool but feeling the exact opposite, I reached inside my pocket, but ended up clumsily thrusting a ring under her nose. Once again, but this time aloud, I said, 'Kekkon shite-kureru?' She turned immediately, smiled and gave me the biggest hug. Then she tried the ring on and hugged me again.

What she didn't do, however, was answer my question.

'Well?' I said anxiously. 'Yes or no?'

'Yes, of course!' she said.

A few days later I had the pleasure of introducing my fiancée to my mother. I was pleased that the two got on so well, as I would need their support in the forthcoming months. To this day Chie has a closer relationship with Mum than I do and makes the effort to stay in touch. It's another reason why I love her.

The good fortune and happiness in my personal life was not being matched in the progress of my father's court case. In May 2005 a Plea and Directions hearing took place at Lincoln Crown Court. I discovered that for technical reasons the thirty-five charges had been reduced to fourteen. My father again pleaded guilty to eight, all involving masturbation. He denied charges 2, 5, 9 and 12, all of which related to oral sex. He also denied two counts of buggery, charges 7 and 14.

Prior to that meeting, DC Smith met me and my mother, sister and fiancée. She wanted to allay any fears we had about giving evidence. In fact she scared us even more.

At no point, I realised, had my family been contacted by the Victim Support team, as promised. We were also confounded by the officer's response to our questions about Dad's suicide note. 'There is no suicide note,' Smith insisted. 'I said we had seized some insurance documents from your father's house. I never mentioned a note.'

I was all right, I had been preparing for this fight for two years. But I was concerned about the effects of these contradictions on my mother and sister. I needed to be strong to go through with the trial, but I also needed to be strong for them. They hadn't asked for this fight.

Just as we began to despair of the 'system' that was

controlling our lives, I was contacted by Jessie Boucher of the Crown Prosecution Service witness care team. She noticed several anomalies in our 'care' and sought to correct them. I had never met a Family Liaison Officer or seen a Victim's Personal Statement, let alone filled one in. The statement is an individual's opportunity to express how much damage he or she has suffered. It is handed to the judge before sentencing. I never had the opportunity to fill one in.

Another person who was happy to be on 'my side' was Shy Keenan, who runs Phoenix Survivors, the internet-based support group for victims of sexual abuse. She contacted the Chief Constable of Devon/Cornwall – he had previously helped her in another case.

I requested another meeting with DC Gooch, who arrived with a colleague, DC Christian. I reported my fears that my case was not being pursued adequately with regard to the other potential abusers and their victims, and mentioned the advice I had been given. He listened to what I had to say but was unmoved.

I personally tracked down a couple of names from the list of sixteen I remembered from my father's past. They had not yet been approached by the police. They also confirmed my worst fears: that I was not the only person to have been abused by this monster. One of the men, who wishes to remain anonymous, admitted that he had been a regular victim. The other man refused to comment.

I promised both men that action was being taken. That while I had a breath left in my body, my father would be brought to justice.

DC Gooch made me aware that any sign of 'rocking the boat' would play into my father's hands. His defence team would make the most of it and possibly get the case dismissed. 'There are things we can't tell you now that we'll happily share after it's over,' I was promised. 'You'll get a full debrief.'

That seemed a long way off. First I had to get through the trial.

After five glorious months, Chie flew back to Japan at the end of June. She had offered to stay for longer, to help me through the trial, but I needed to be selfish and focus on the case. With her gone, I spent the summer working at Eton College, teaching the children of élite members of the Chinese Communist Party. The job distracted me during the day. At night I was too aware of the impending pressure. 'Can I go through with it?' I wondered. Regular e-mails from Chie and words of encouragement from my local friends told me that I could. 'Think of that young lad in Grantham,' I reminded myself. That was all the impetus I needed.

I wasn't the only one who needed support, however. Brenda Fairhurst, my mother, was soon to testify against her husband of twenty-seven years. Despite all my misgivings about her past treatment of me, I know this was a daunting prospect for her. My sister Jo was living with a friend and popped by when she could, but it was important that Mum had company, I felt, in the run-up to the trial. When my time at Eton College came to an end, and with a month to go until the court case, I decided to move in with Mum.

As the trial date drew closer, my mother seemed to become more anxious to talk to me about her life, and more than ever before she disclosed many of her longest held secrets. She talked, for example, about her sex life. I asked her to stop because it was embarrassing for me to hear, but she needed to get things off her chest. Clearly worries about the court case and possible cross-examination were preying on her mind. It was as though she wanted me to know everything before I heard her give evidence.

19

That Game Stops Here

On 6 September 2005 the case of the Crown versus Clifford John Fairhurst commenced.

I turned up in the morning as instructed, while Mum stayed at home. As a fellow witness, she was not allowed to see my testimony in case it influenced her recall of events. I had plenty of support from my friends. Richard, Big Dave, Big Ste, Biker Daz, Dave and Bushy Paul were all present and correct. It meant everything to see their supportive faces and giant frames in the spectator stands.

Lincoln Court is housed within the grounds of the city's medieval castle. It really is an imposing building, and breath-taking if you're a sightseer passing through. If you have anything to do with one of the cases, however, its beauty becomes quite intimidating. I felt cowed by its grandeur as I approached the court along the cobbled entrance.

Not everyone is affected in the same way. On our way into the building, my support posse and I caught a glimpse of Dad arriving with members of his family. He was laughing and joking as if he was taking everyone on a picnic at the castle. I had borrowed a suit for the day, on the advice of the police solicitor. My father was dressed in a polo shirt and a pair of unironed trousers. He looked like an extra from *Steptoe and Son*. 'He still doesn't get it,' I thought. 'He hasn't got a clue.'

The first day was a complete anticlimax. The previous case overran and we were all sent home with nothing even started. At ten o'clock the following morning I took the stand. Under guidance from my barrister I told the court in graphic detail everything that had happened to me all those years ago. We went through the police statement sentence by sentence and the gallery watched in silence. As I spoke, I saw the foreman of the jury shake his head. I don't think he liked what he was hearing.

I didn't dare look at my father as I spoke, in case he put me off. But my friends told me afterwards that he had looked everywhere except at me. It was almost as though I wasn't there.

They also said he seemed to smile occasionally, as if to show I had got it wrong. He was patronising me, trying to bully me still, to make me feel that what I was doing was wrong and that what he said was right. He'd managed that for so many years, but no more. 'That game stops here,' I thought.

When Dad's barrister stood up to cross-examine me, I was glad of the friendly faces staring down from the spectators' area. As expected, I was portrayed as a drug addict and a liar. The defence case appeared to hinge on the idea that I was trying to blackmail my father for his money. Perhaps that would have been plausible ten years ago but these days my dad lived in squalor in a tiny council flat.

I was only rattled by one question. 'Were you aware that your father has had a procedure on his penis called a "Dawson's Slit" that makes it painful for him to have penetrative intercourse?' I was asked.

'I don't understand that term,' I replied. 'But it can't be that painful considering that he seemed to enjoy penetrating me.'

The trial was halted after my evidence. Apparently new information had come to light. The police had found another victim. It was Robert, the son of Dad's old colleague John.

The trial started again the next day.

When the new jury's foreman revealed he had a relative who was abused it was scrapped once more. Finally, at the fourth time of asking, I was called into the witness box again.

I was asked once more about the Dawson's Slit procedure. This time I was ready.

'Do you mean, did I know my father is circumcised?' I replied. 'Of course I did. I saw his penis almost every day for ten years.'

The defence barrister was confused. 'In the last trial you stated you were not aware of it,' she said.

'I didn't understand your terminology,' I explained, 'so I looked it up on the internet.'

Her job was to make me look like an unreliable witness, but after ten years of preparation, I had the advantage.

I also had the strength of my mates in the gallery and beyond. Chie had sent me a lock of her hair, which I wore in my breast pocket every day.

Not everyone was on my side, however. As I made my way back towards the witness waiting room, one of my dad's family was waiting for me in the corridor. 'You're a nasty piece of work, you are,' she spat out at me. 'When this is over you'll fucking pay, I promise you.' For a second I didn't know what to do as she stood in front of me cackling. My breath was taken away.

The next thing I knew, my friend Daz had leapt between us

and started to put her straight in language she would understand. A few moments later a couple of court orderlies intervened and warned my relative that intimidating a witness carried a prison sentence. One more step out of line and she would be ejected from the court.

Robert was called to the stand the next day. He gave his evidence via video link, but he was still obviously very nervous. I sat ten feet away from my father as the television monitors played out the latest part of the drama. Dad didn't look at me once, but I spent a lot of time that afternoon, as I did every day during the trial, trying to drill holes in the back of his head with my eyes. I told him what he had done to me, what the effects were and how I felt. I said everything to him that I should have said to his face years ago. If he was telepathic, he heard me.

I watched Robert's testimony with interest. Over the last few weeks I had believed the trial was only about me, but I remembered now that others had suffered too. Robert's story was troublingly similar to mine. Things I thought only I knew, he had experienced as well. He was abused in a truck when Dad let him drive, for example. The exact same thing had happened to me.

Dad didn't flinch as he listened to Robert, just as he'd remained unfazed in front of me. As witness after witness stood up to help paint a picture of this pathetic and untrustworthy character, he just smiled knowingly. It was as though he were attending a theatrical production where the audience sits among the cast. He was to all intents and purposes an interested bystander. If he appreciated how serious his situation really was, he didn't let on. He looked as if he knew he would win. He had the arrogance of a gambler who had fixed

the race. More than once I started to worry about his composure. 'What if he knows something I don't?' I fretted. But how
could he?

The only witness I could not watch was my mother. While
she was interrogated I sat on a grass verge outside the court
and listened to my iPod. Radiohead were constant companions at that time.

Dad took the stand at the end of the week. My barrister had
told me that things seemed to be going in our favour, but from
the look on my father's face throughout the trial I was worried
he had something up his sleeve. Something was giving him the
confidence to sit there like visiting royalty. But what?

When the call came, my dad approached the dock like an
actor taking to the stage. He was still smiling, still holding his
head proudly, still radiating confidence that he was innocent,
that somehow it was all a big mistake. A big joke.

A few minutes later it was a very different man standing
before me.

I had never seen the law work at this level before. I had
certainly never been on the prosecution side. My barrister was
very impressive and made every word count. With each
sentence he either set my father up to incriminate himself
or verbally crushed him with fact. I knew the verdict could
still go Dad's way, but from where I was sitting it was like
watching the lions released on the Christians. Blow after blow
rained down on him, and he seemed to have nothing to give
back. I couldn't help smiling inside as each answer seemed to
trip him up more.

One early exchange saw my barrister challenge something
Dad had said in his police statement when he was arrested.

In reply to the question 'Did Duncan ever see you ejaculate?' he had said, 'Well, yes – no – I wouldn't let it get that far, I would always hide that from him.' The police officer had then posed the same question again. This time he answered, 'He saw once. I would hide it from him. Usually it never went that far.'

Now my barrister addressed Dad directly.

'Duncan says you made him masturbate you two or three times a week. Is that correct?'

'No,' came the reply.

'Well, in your own figures then, how often did you ask Duncan to masturbate you?'

'Once or twice a month, once mostly but occasionally twice a month,' my father said.

'Again by your own account, how long did this behaviour continue?' the barrister enquired.

'For five years.'

'Did you ejaculate?'

'Yes.'

I saw my barrister's eyes flicker. It was time for the killer blow.

'In your police statement,' he began, 'under oath, you stated that Duncan only made you ejaculate once. Today in court under oath again, by your own admission, Mr Fairhurst, using your figures not mine, you have admitted in effect that Duncan was made to masturbate you and indeed brought you to orgasm on sixty occasions over a five-year period.'

Dad had no choice but to admit it.

There was an audible gasp in the courtroom. I could see my supporters in the gallery all leaning forward in case they missed a word. If I hadn't been so nervous I would have enjoyed the drama.

'I put it to you, Mr Fairhurst,' said the barrister, 'that everything you have said in court today is absolute nonsense.'

Watching this mismatched contest unfold, I was finally able to relax. I had never seen anyone talk to my father like that. I don't think anyone ever had. I'd certainly never dared, even after all I'd been through. I was tongue-tied in front of him when it came to anything close to emotions. Mum had yelled at him often enough, but not about this. Not about anything important. I remembered how he had beaten her once or twice. For all her volume and critical words, I'm sure she knew not to overstep her mark.

But now, here in Lincoln Court in front of witnesses, my father was finally meeting his match. He was up against someone he couldn't bully. And I really don't think he knew what to do.

By way of deflecting the accusations of buggery, my father said he'd lifted me, aged ten, into the bath, and his penis had accidentally come into contact in 'a non-sexual way' with my anus. This proved too much for the listening judge.

'Mr Fairhurst, did your son really need to be lifted into the bath at ten years old?' he asked. 'Why were you naked? And please describe for the court how your penis touched your son's anus in a "non-sexual" way?'

My barrister also queried my father's explanation of how, after swimming, he would still dry my genitals thoroughly, even though I was old enough to do it alone. 'Are you telling the court that you still had to towel dry your son who was by this time eight or nine years old?' he asked.

'Yes,' my father answered. 'That's just what we did.'

'I doubt it,' my barrister said. 'That's just what *you* did, isn't it, Mr Fairhurst?'

Dad's defence, when it came, was intricately woven but it appeared to hinge on one fact: the vehicles Robert and I claimed to have been abused in were not consistent with the ones he had owned at the time.

In a nutshell, we were liars because at the time we said he was driving a 7.5-ton truck, he actually owned a 3-ton model.

Just when I thought his testimony couldn't get any more bizarre, he failed to produce a key lease agreement. The paperwork submitted to the court had one registration number crossed out and a new one written in Dad's handwriting.

With the defence concluded soon after, it was just a question of waiting for a verdict. My crew and I sat around for the rest of the afternoon waiting for the call to return to the court, but it didn't come that day.

The tension in all of us was apparent, and later that day, back at my mother's house, she and I let it spill over into a very unpleasant argument. We had started talking about Dad, as usual, and got on to the subject of Jo warning her that my father was abusing me. I asked her once again to explain why she hadn't taken Jo seriously, but she refused to go over it again. I lost my temper, but she had the final word. 'You get more like your bloody father every day,' she shouted at me. 'If living here is so hard, why don't you move in with him and see how you like that.'

I couldn't believe what I was hearing. To be told I was like the man who had ruined my life was bad enough. But following that with the command to move in with him killed my respect for my mother. The last couple of years had been great, probably our best ever as mother and son. But all the good times we'd had recently were forgotten there and then. There was no way I could spend another night in that house.

The jury returned on 19 September. Before we went in, my group of supporters was cautioned by court staff not to say anything or start a fuss. 'Try to look dignified,' we were instructed.

The judge addressed the foreman of the jury. 'Have you reached a majority verdict?' he asked.

'Yes, we have,' came the response.

The court clerk read out each charge. After every single one the foreman said the same word: 'Guilty'.

The time seemed to pass in slow motion. I could not believe what I was hearing. I had won. After twenty years, I had won.

In front of me I saw my dad visibly wither. The bravura that had concerned me throughout the week had vanished. I saw him tremble as he contemplated the judge's words. When he sat down he seemed smaller. Either that or his chair had grown.

The court was adjourned for half an hour while the judge considered the appropriate punishment. The result was hard to take in at first. For each count of masturbation my father was sentenced to two years' imprisonment. For each count of oral sex, he got four and a half years. Each charge of buggery carried a sentence of nine years. Total time: fifty-two years.

I was disappointed to learn that these terms would run concurrently. In other words my father would serve only nine years – less than the period of time during which he abused me.

For offences committed against Robert he was sentenced to a further two-and-a-half years.

As the sentence was announced, Dad went so red that I could suddenly see his scalp burning underneath his full covering of snow-white hair. Everything glowed, from his ears to his cheeks to his forehead. He looked either very angry or very embarrassed.

As my father struggled to comprehend what was happening, the judge barked, 'Take him down.' Previously during breaks in proceedings, Dad had been led very courteously by a guard down the stairs from the dock. This time he was spun round to face the gallery, where we were all watching from, his hands were cuffed tightly and he was physically bundled out of the room.

Not once did he look up. The swagger of earlier in the week had disappeared. He was a broken man.

As my father was led away, Big Dave called out, 'Have fun in the prison showers, you piece of shit.' I didn't say anything, but inside I was smiling.

I was on cloud nine as I left the court. Each official I passed congratulated me on my performance. One or two remarked on the dignity I had shown. 'You've no idea how hard it was,' I said.

As we funnelled out of the room, I was aware of a face staring at me. It was the same relative who'd screamed abuse at me before. 'What the fuck are you looking at?' she hissed.

I ignored her. She had already been warned for trying to intimidate me before I gave evidence.

'It's not over, you know,' she shouted at me.

I said nothing but I wanted to. I wanted to shout in her face. I wanted to yell, 'Of course it's over, you stupid cow! My father is on his way to prison for more than a decade. He pleaded guilty to eight charges and was found guilty on all the others as well. In his own words he abused children. Do you support paedophiles? Do you think grown men should be able to abuse their kids?'

Most of my supporters and Robert's family went to a pub across the road from the castle. It was more of a wake than a celebration, but there was a mood of solidarity in the air that needed to be observed. My mother and Robert's father were inseparable for the afternoon as they compared stories. My sister didn't attend the verdict. She preferred to work that day, in order to maintain some semblance of normality in her life. When I spoke to her later she was as relieved as I was with the result.

While the rest of the gallery filtered away, Big Dave and I stayed behind. The first thing I wanted to do was call Chie and let her know the verdict. I knew she would be at work, but I happily chatted to her answering machine for a few minutes before signing off. Then Dave and I climbed the path around the castle wall. We had talked about this moment for several days. It gave us the perfect vantage-point to see the comings and goings at the court gates. More important, we could be seen clearly by anyone passing through.

I don't know if he saw us or not, but as the van carrying my father passed, Dave and I stood and waved. The blacked-out windows hid him from sight, but I suspect he saw us. I hope so. I hope he saw us wave. I hope he regarded it as a gesture of victory.

My father was going to prison.

I had won.

EPILOGUE

I Knew it was Over

There's a saying that goes, 'Good things come to those who wait.' I waited twenty years for justice. My father was sent down on 19 September 2005. He was sentenced to a total of fifty-two years in prison, with each individual penalty set to run concurrently. He would be out in under a dozen.

I should have been the happiest man on Earth. But justice came at a price. During the trial I learned things I wish I'd never known. Although we got a conviction, the investigation left a bad taste in my mouth. My father pleaded guilty to several offences from the point of his arrest and was labeled an 'active paedophile' by the police, yet he was bailed by the magistrate's and Crown court, despite the police seeking a remand judgment in both hearings.

A lot of my anger and frustration is directed not only at the police but at the system that sets the rules they must follow. My father got legal advice from the moment he was arrested, he was able to consult his lawyer whenever he chose. I could not. When it came to challenging the conduct of the police investigation, we were not allowed any legal aid for our own lawyers on the grounds that we might be coached by them.

What about the possibility of my father being coached by his lawyers?

It seems to me that the UK system is stacked in favour of the criminal and against the victim. The defence talked about my father's rights during the trial, but what about my own rights as a child? My right to grow without fear? My right to find and develop my own sexuality with a consenting partner of my choosing? These things are priceless and can never be returned to me. But I did fight for my rights and although the trigger for the disclosure of my abuse was seeing my father with the young boy that day in Grantham, I now realise that that was also the point when I finally regained control of my life. That was when I stopped being a victim and started being a survivor.

We all do things we regret. In my life I have lied to the people I loved most to prevent them getting too close. I have stolen and cheated. I have been involved in drugs transactions to the tune of £1,000,000 over the last few decades. None of us is without blame. But I have moved on. I've put the shackles of my past behind me.

A month after the trial finished, I moved to Hiroshima to teach English. Chie and I married in Japan on 25 December 2005. 'I don't want you to be scared of Christmas any more,' she told me. 'I want you to celebrate, like everyone else.'

One day my wife and I will have children. I swear now that I will treat them with respect and love. They will not have to endure anything that I went through.

I am grateful for each day now. I have my education behind me, and I am making a difference to the lives of many who come to my classes. Occasionally I think of those days back in Lincoln. The stealing, the dealing, the drug-taking. Many of my acquaintances from that time are still leading the same pointless existence. Some, like me, have moved on. A handful have died.

'There but for the grace of God . . .'

Each day that passes brings with it new pleasures in a foreign land with a partner who loves me. Each night, however, reminds me of the terrors I can never fully shake off.

Nightmares fill my every sleeping hour, just as they did when I was a kid. In them I see my father, sometimes as himself, sometimes as a spider, sometimes as a shark. A recurring theme is me watching helplessly as he abuses a child. I never know the victim, but I know the pain the young stranger endures.

When I arrived in Hiroshima after the trial I felt renewed. I was born again. I had finally shed the skin of my past and I was ready to move forwards. There was just one thing I had to do to complete the grieving process.

During the build-up to the trial, I did not cry once. I did not cry when I heard the evidence from my father's other victim. I did not cry when I discovered that my mother had betrayed my trust.

A month after landing in Japan I found myself playing the same two Radiohead tracks on repeat on my iPod.

For the first time the enormity of what I had been through hit me. With 'Lucky' and 'Karma Police' playing over and over again, I hugged my legs under my arms and sobbed my heart out. I cried until I had no tears left.

Chie found me curled in a ball in the darkness, covered in snot and tear stains. She cuddled me and held me tight.

I knew then that it was over.